UNDERSTANDING YOUR DOG

UNDERSTANDING YOUR DOG

A New Approach to Training

PETER GRIFFITHS

DAVID & CHARLES
NEWTON ABBOT LONDON
NORTH POMFRET (VT) VERMONT

ISBN 0 7153 7353 6

© Peter Griffiths 1977

All rights reserved. No part of this publication may be reproduced, stored in a retrieval system, or transmitted, in any form or by any means, electronic, mechanical, photocopying, recording or otherwise, without the prior permission of David & Charles (Publishers) Limited

Set in 11 on 13pt Baskerville
by A. E. Smith (Printers) Limited
and printed in Great Britain
by Biddles Limited Guildford
for David & Charles (Publishers) Limited
Brunel House Newton Abbot Devon

Published in the United States of America
by David & Charles Inc
North Pomfret Vermont 05053 USA

Published in Canada
by Douglas David & Charles Limited
1875 Welch Street North Vancouver BC

CONTENTS

		Page
	Author's Preface	7
1	Dogs in the Wild	9
2	The Domesticated Dog	19
3	Canine Behaviour	32
4	Training, the Man/Dog Relationship	44
5	The Primary Aids	60
6	Elementary Training	72
7	Further Training	82
8	The Sheepdog	92
	Index	107

AUTHOR'S PREFACE

Improvisation plays an important part in any programme of dog training. Every dog is an individual and a training technique that succeeds with one animal may fail completely with another. Dogs have a knack of doing the unexpected and will find loopholes in the most comprehensive and carefully prepared training schedule. The best any author can do is to suggest certain approaches that are sometimes useful in teaching a particular exercise. For the rest the handler must rely on his knowledge of dogs in general, and his own dog in particular, to evolve an effective training programme. Thus it is very important that the handler should have some idea of the workings of the canine mind. For this reason a considerable part of this book is devoted to a study of dog psychology.

My wife, Mary, and I own two bitches. Debbie, our year-old Dobermann, is a big, greedy, boisterous clown of an animal. In contrast Kim, our two-year-old Border collie, is a much quieter, more sensitive creature. They will make frequent appearances in this book as I use them to illustrate various aspects of canine behaviour.

As well as inheriting the physical traits of its ancestors an animal also derives certain mental qualities. Such inherited mental characteristics are termed instincts. Although slightly altered by selective breeding the instincts of a domestic dog bear a very close resemblance to those of its wild ancestors. Hence a study of the instincts and behaviour of dogs in the wild state gives us an insight into the mentality of the domestic animal. Understanding a dog is an essential prerequisite for its successful training. This book describes the nature and origins of the canine instincts and suggests how best to use this knowledge to expedite a dog's upbringing.

In the latter part of the book practical training methods are discussed. In this context flexibility is very important. If the handler finds that a certain method of instruction is making little impression upon his dog he should alter his approach. It is for this reason that I have suggested two or three teaching techniques for each of the more difficult exercises. The handler should select that approach which he considers will best suit the temperament of his dog. Sometimes he will find that a combination or alternation of methods is the most effective. If all this fails, and sometimes it will, the handler should improvise a technique of his own. In so doing he will be greatly assisted by a rudimentary knowledge of canine psychology. The relevant material will be found in the earlier chapters of this book.

1
DOGS IN THE WILD

The training of any dog is greatly facilitated if the handler has a rudimentary knowledge of the animal's natural instincts. This necessarily involves a consideration of the dog in its wild state. The prime function of such a study, discussed in practical detail in later chapters, is to supply the handler with sufficient information to enable him to formulate an intelligent, flexible, personal training system. So in my first chapter I will take a brief look at the life and behaviour of wild dogs in their natural habitat.

Although there are exceptions (like the fox and the coyote) the majority of wild dogs, including wolves, jackals and Cape hunting dogs, are pack animals. Their lives and personalities depend to a large extent upon the influence of their fellow pack members. Even the modern domestic animal will alter its personality in the presence of other dogs: its previously suppressed natural impulses such as aggression, lust, and the hunting instinct come to the fore, and it becomes wilder and less controllable. Sometimes a number of domestic animals will consistently hunt together; whilst in a pack they will revert to a semi-wild state and will roam the countryside killing and mutilating scores of sheep and lambs. Most farmers will shoot such dogs on sight — and who can blame them! Yet in most cases the individual members of such a pack are normal, healthy, intelligent animals. Much of the responsibility lies with the dogs' owners, because they have failed to administer the necessary training, discipline and supervision.

A dog pack is governed by a system of hierarchical dominance, in which four general rules are observed. A strong dog dominates a weaker one. A large dog dominates a smaller one. A mature dog will dominate a younger dog of comparable size and strength. A bitch will dominate a dog of comparable size and strength (this stems from the fact that a dog has natural inhibitions about biting a bitch—a phenomenon that persists in the domestic animal). There are, of course, exceptions to these rules arising from individual bravery, aggression, roughness, cowardice and so on. Recent observations on the Cape hunting dog have revealed that, in this particular species, the male and female animals have their own separate hierarchies.

Once a pack member's rank has been decided it is very long lasting. Occasionally a younger dog will endeavour to depose a superior. The instinct for social order is so strong, however, that the rebellious youngster will delay its coup until it is considerably more powerful than its ageing senior. Sometimes a pack leader will become old and infirm and a younger dog will make a successful challenge for the pack's leadership. If the deposed leader survives its wounds it may rejoin the pack accepting a lower rank. Frequently though, the old leader will leave the pack and become a 'lone wolf'.

An adult dog may threaten a young puppy but will never actually attack it. The mature animal has natural inhibitions about biting a puppy. But how does an adult dog recognise a puppy? Size cannot be the criterion otherwise an adult dachshund would have no qualms about attacking a young Dobermann. Neither can appearance, because the various different breeds encompass a fantastic diversity of form. An adult dog recognises a youngster by the latter's characteristic behaviour. If a puppy feels that its safety is in jeopardy it instinctively adopts a submissive posture. It rolls onto its back exposing its throat and belly to possible attack. Often it will pass a few drops of urine which its aggressor sniffs inquisitively. A display of this kind evokes the adult dog's natural inhibitions about attacking a puppy.

Puppyish appeasement gestures frequently persist into

adulthood. The day-to-day life of any social animal will involve numerous minor disputes. The dog pack is no exception. If every little quarrel escalated into a serious fight many pack members would be killed or incapacitated. In actual fact the majority of intrapack conflicts are almost bloodless. The subordinate dog is very quickly impressed by its rival's show of aggression and hurriedly adopts a submissive posture. The display of appeasement of a vanquished adult is strikingly similar to the submissive deportment of a young puppy, and it has the same effect. It arouses inhibitions in the dominant dog and causes it to discontinue its attack. The fight ends without unnecessary bloodshed. Sometimes the defeated dog will try to lick the lips of its conqueror (the origin of this particular submissive gesture is discussed later in the chapter).

An unpleasant aspect of pack behaviour is the instinct for healthy pack members to gang up on and kill their weak, senile or infirm fellows. Yet natural selection has good reason for favouring this instinct. It removes deleterious genes from the population and ensures that every member pulls its weight in the pack's vital activities. Unlike human society, a canine community cannot afford to support inactive members. This instinct occasionally manifests itself where domestic dogs are kept in large numbers, and results in the most horrible kennel fights.

Though not above scavenging if the opportunity arises, wild dogs are primarily hunters. A predator must first of all locate its prey, and to do so the dog relies heavily on its prodigious sense of smell. It is difficult to imagine the sensitivity of a dog's nose. The animal's olfactory membrane registers as many sensory impressions as the retina of a human eye. Deprive a man of his sense of smell and he is little inconvenienced — but take away his sight! To a wild dog the loss of either of these senses would be equally calamitous. A few facts. The human nasal cavity includes an olfactory area of five square centimetres comprising five million olfactory cells. An Alsatian dog has two hundred and twenty million olfactory cells on an olfactory membrane one hundred and fifty square centimetres in area. As if this were not enough, tests with an olfactometer have revealed that the Alsatian's olfactory cells are considerably more sensitive than man's. All in all, a dog's sense of smell is one million times more efficient than our own.

A dog tracking its prey utilises two factors: the scent of its quarry either on the ground, or carried to it on the wind; and the smell of the trail of crushed plants and microorganisms which the pursued animal has trampled. This second factor explains why a dog tracks better over grass and vegetation than over bare soil or rock. An animal's scent originates from an odorous sweaty substance comprising a mixture of fatty acids. Different animals exude different concentrations of the various fatty acids. Thus a wild dog is able to distinguish the trail of its quarry from that of other, less appetising, creatures. Even individual animals of the same species release the fatty acids in slightly varying proportions. It is this fact that enables a police dog to differentiate the trail of a suspect from a jungle of distracting traces. A man walking barefoot loses about one quarter of a billionth of a gram of sweat every step. This minute weight represents several million molecules and is easily sufficient for a keen-nosed dog to detect. If the man puts on a pair of shoes the majority of his scent is contained. Even so, over a million molecules of fatty acids pass through the shoe-leather with every step, a quantity well within the powers of detection of a trained tracker dog.

When a wild dog encounters the trail of an animal on which it preys, there are two directions in which it can follow the trail. One way takes it towards its quarry, the other leads in precisely the opposite direction. The dog bases its decision on the fact that the individual fatty acids comprising the scent trail evaporate at different speeds. This means that as the trail ages its smell becomes very slightly altered. The canine nose is acute enough to detect this subtle difference — so once again the dog's phenomenal sense of smell helps the animal locate its intended victim.

A hunting dog does not, however, rely solely on its sense of smell. The smaller wild dogs like the jackal, the coyote and the fox spend much of their time hunting rabbits, rats, mice, voles, snakes and even insects. Such small game has little scent and conceals itself in long grass and other vegetation. To hunt prey of this kind the dog relies largely on its sense of hearing. It stands immobile, ears pricked, waiting for an incautious movement, a rustle of grass perhaps, to reveal its quarry's location. The dog bounds swiftly towards the sound with its nose and forelegs held close together. If the manoeuvre is successful its quarry is crushed and straight away devoured. This technique of hunting is occasionally to be observed in the domestic dog.

Canine vision is not particularly well developed and is relatively little used by the dog in seeking out its prey. For many years scientists have disagreed as to whether or not the dog possesses colour vision. It is safe to say, though, that if the animal *is* able to distinguish colours it can only do so to a very limited extent. Experiments on police dogs in Germany demonstrated the fallibility of the canine sense of sight, showing that the dogs had little idea of their master's form and features but recognised him largely by the clothes that he wore. Every dog mistook a complete stranger for its master when the former was wearing its master's clothing. When the dog's master swapped only his overcoat with a stranger, eighteen of the twenty-one police dogs followed the stranger! In another experiment the majority of the dogs failed to pick out their master when he sat naked in the company of several other naked men.

The African wild dogs do occasionally use their vision to locate their prey. Often a jackal or a Cape hunting dog will cast a quick glance skyward as it goes about its business. In most cases the dog learns nothing from this exercise; but now and again it is rewarded by the sight of a flock of circling vultures, a sure indication of a dead or dying animal. In such a case the dog will straightaway set off towards the vultures —

and its prospective dinner!

The dog is not a nocturnal animal. Compared to members of the cat family its night vision is very poor. For this reason wild dogs confine their hunting expeditions to the early morning, late evening and moonlit nights. Hunting is largely a co-operative venture. Even jackals, normally solitary animals, form themselves into packs of six or seven to hunt gazelle. The hunting party selects a weak, ailing or injured animal as its quarry and wears it down by sheer persistence. This contrasts with the hunting technique of the cat family which involves short spurts of tremendous speed and power. A pack of Cape hunting dogs will pursue its prey, gazelle, warthog, wildebeeste or zebra, for up to four miles at an average speed of about thirty miles an hour (occasionally the pace quickens to nearly forty miles an hour!). If after this distance their quarry still eludes them the dogs abandon the chase. About fifty per cent of their hunting expeditions proceed to a successful conclusion. When the leading dog overtakes its prey it grasps it by its throat or hind leg. This slows the animal down and it is soon surrounded by the rest of the pack. The dogs kill their quarry by disembowelling—a process that takes about two minutes.

The jackal is one of the smaller members of the dog family, about the size of a fox. Yet a hungry jackal will tackle a full grown zebra, a feat scarcely compatible with the animal's (undeserved) reputation for cowardice! The largest wild dog, the wolf, preys mainly on deer. At one time it hunted the buffalo herds that roamed the North American continent. When man's activities caused the extinction of these herds the wolf turned its attention towards livestock. Not unnaturally the animal became very unpopular and was, and still is, quite severely persecuted.

After making a kill the dogs gorge; then follow two or three days fasting until their next kill. The wild dog's metabolism is geared to occasional meals of enormous bulk. It follows, then, that the domestic animal will be healthier if fed in a similar fashion. Yet when it comes to feeding their pets many dog owners make the mistake of anthropomorphism — they insist that because man thrives on a very regular pattern of eating, then so will a dog. They disregard the fact that man's natural eating habits are very different from those of a dog. Man, of course, is a primate — a highly advanced member of the ape family. In the wild state the herbivorous members of this family spend most of their waking life continually nibbling at fruit, nuts and other foodstuffs. So while it is perfectly natural for a man to eat four or five meals a day, it is very unnatural for a dog. An adult dog should be fed once a day and any food that it does not consume immediately should be taken away. All animals are greedy; and if a half-eaten bowl of food is left lying around the house a normal dog will eat much more than is good for it. Too many dogs (and too many humans) are overweight. Yet many dog owners actively encourage healthy, alert, dignified animals to eat themselves into sick, ugly, pathetic balls of fat. In nature the dog that gulped its food fastest got the most; its chances of survival were increased. Dogs rarely trouble to chew their food, they bolt it whole and rely on their incredibly robust stomachs slowly to digest it between successive meals. Greed and selfishness are instincts that nature has favoured in every animal — the greediest and most selfish were the most successful in the struggle for survival.

The diet of a wild dog includes a considerable quantity of vegetable matter. Sometimes this is consumed in its raw state (domestic dogs often nibble at grass) but often it originates from the stomach and intestines of the herbivores that constitute a wild dog's prey. Vegetable matter is an important constituent of a dog's diet since the B vitamins contained therein assist the formation of healthy nerve tissue. Unbleached tripe (raw cow stomach), available from many butchers, is an excellent and inexpensive dog food and is a balanced diet in itself. Many farmers feed their dogs on little else, and the animals thrive. Unfortunately raw tripe is somewhat unpleasant in both smell and appearance — during the summer months it attracts flies and quickly turns putrid. More squeamish dog owners may prefer to supplement their pets' protein intake with the occasional egg. Biscuits, milk and two raw eggs make a most nutritious and inexpensive meal: a welcome change from the almost inevitable menu of tinned meat and biscuits. Foodstuffs to avoid are such starchy, sugary commodities as potato, cake, sweets, white bread, untoasted brown bread and so on. A familiar catalogue! A wild dog devours an appreciable quantity of raw animal hide which has an abrasive action on the animal's intestine causing the displacement of parasitic worms. At one time vets recommended the use of chopped rabbit skin as a cure for worms; nowadays there are many brands of proprietary worm pills which do the job even more effectively.

A wild dog buries any food, particularly bones, in excess of its immediate requirements. This has the advantage of protecting the food from carrion-eaters like eagles and vultures. Because buried food gives off little scent it is less likely to be discovered by rival dogs. In times of hunger, or when a rival is in the vicinity, the dog will dig up any food that it has placed in cache. The dog remembers roughly where the food is buried and relies on its scent to locate it exactly. If the scent is very faint the food is sometimes lost. The instinct to bury food has persisted in the domestic dog — as many a gardener knows to his cost.

Wild dogs like the wolf and jackal are only pack animals for part of the year. In the spring dog and bitch pair up and leave the pack to mate. Unlike the domestic bitch a wild bitch only comes into season once a year. A pair of wolves mate for life and show touching faithfulness towards one another. In the presence of her mate a wolf bitch is all adoration and submissiveness (in spite of the fact that the dog never physically exerts his dominance). And the wolf dog, unlike his philandering domesticated descendent, is strictly monogamous. If his mate dies he does not remate but remains a widower for the rest of his life. Prior to mating a pair of wild dogs establish an area of domestic territory of about three acres. The two animals mark their territorial boundaries with their urine and drive off any intruders with the utmost ferocity. A male fox even goes to the extent of marking his mate with urine to warn off other foxes.

Howling is another means by which a wild dog may advertise its territorial claims. Howling ceremonies are particularly common in the case of the wolf and the jackal. Wild dogs never bark however; barking is a canine characteristic which only seems to appear following domestication.

Other wild animals have similar idiosyncracies by which they mark out their territories. Wild rabbits are so often observed scratching their chins that at one time they were thought to suffer from mange. But after careful observation an Australian biologist proved that this action was territorially motivated. He discovered that a rabbit's chin is overspread with numerous sweat glands. When the animal scratches, the scented secretions of these glands adhere to the soles of its feet and the rabbit treads this odorous substance throughout the length and breadth of its territory; its characteristic smell acts as a deterrent to other rabbits. The brown bear habitually rubs its back and muzzle against rocks, boulders, tree trunks and so on. Like the rabbit this creature was once suspected of mange. Again the allegations of inadequate personal hygiene proved unfounded; it has since been shown that the animal is merely following its territorial instincts. The rubbing ritual leaves a greasy, smelly trail which defines the limits of the bear's territory.

When a wild bitch is about to give birth she seeks out a 'nest'. This may be a small cave, a hole in the ground, a sheltered position between rocks or a hollow log. Different species of dog produce litters of different sizes, but six or seven puppies is an average number. When her puppies are born a bitch performs a series of quite complicated operations, all of them purely instinctive. She tears open the foetal membranes, bites through the puppies' umbilical cords, licks them clean and eats the afterbirth. This last action has greater significance than is apparent at first sight. The afterbirth contains certain chemicals which stimulate the bitch's production of milk. For the first weeks of their lives the puppies feed from their mother. During this period the bitch remains with her pups and her mate supplies food for them both. The puppies are weaned after five or six weeks. Their first solid food takes the form of meat regurgitated by their parents; this system is advantageous in that the food is protected from the attacks of carrion-eaters while it is in transit between the kill and the den. The pups greet their parents with much squealing, tail-wagging and licking. The action of licking their parents' face and lips has the effect of stimulating regurgitation. Welcoming behaviour of this sort continues into adulthood where it is employed as a submissive gesture, and, as an expression of canine greeting and affection, has persisted into domestication.

At the age of three months the puppies are old enough to accompany their parents on hunting expeditions. At five or six months a young dog makes its first kill. At this tender age the young animal is introduced to the intricacies of canine society.

2
THE DOMESTICATED DOG

Natural Selection

The dog's ancestry can be traced back forty million years to a long-tailed, arboreal, civet-like mammal called Miacis — small and relatively unspecialised. In contrast the modern dog is a highly specialised hunting carnivore. How, then, did the dog achieve its high degree of specialisation?

It may be readily observed that no two animals of the same species are identical. This is because the genetic material of any individual animal is minutely different from that of all its contemporaries. Every mental and physical characteristic of an animal is precisely determined by its genetic material (or 'genes'), the elements in the chemical make-up of the animal which are passed on from parents to offspring. The chemical components of an animal's genes are complex; should a slight change occur in the chemical make-up of any one gene, the animal will be characterised by a physical or mental feature different from its forbears. This chemical change is called a 'mutation', and can happen at any time; the number of mutations and the form they take is quite random — but once a mutation has occurred it is self-perpetuating.

Most mutations are deleterious and the animal bearing them either dies or fails to produce any offspring. In either case the mutant gene dies out along with the animal carrying it, and natural selection can be said to have operated against this particular mutant gene.

Other mutations, perhaps one in a hundred, are not deleterious but produce slightly altered genes which have no effect on the survival of their carrier. An example might be a mutant gene which produced a slight change in the colouring of an animal's coat. In this case the animal survives to pass the new gene on to its offspring and natural selection operates neither in its favour, nor against it.

In a few, very rare cases a mutant gene may be produced which *increases* the survival value of its carrier. Here natural selection will operate in favour of the new gene. Consider a pack of primitive dogs; dogs that do not display the extreme specialisation apparent in our modern animal. A mutant gene may arise in one of the pack members causing, say, a slight strengthening of the animal's jaw muscles. In consequence, this dog and its offspring will stand a slightly better chance of making a kill when hunting. Thus in times of food shortage, this strain of dogs will survive at the expense of some of the less well adapted pack members.

The same dogs will be slightly better adapted to win any intrapack disputes. Their social position will permit them to mate more frequently than weaker animals of lower rank (who are sometimes not allowed to mate at all). So dogs with the mutant gene for strong jaws will produce more than their fair share of offspring. This ensures that successive generations of wild dogs contain more and more animals with powerful jaws. Specialisation is, therefore, favoured by natural selection.

The concept of natural selection is frequently explained in terms of 'survival of the fittest'. This is an excellent expression provided that one bears in mind the biologist's definition of 'fitness'. To the biologist a 'fit' animal is one which is well adapted to live its own style of life, in its own particular environment. Thus the dog, a carnivore, is fitter for having strong jaws. Powerful jaws, however, would be of no survival value to an animal which has specialised as a vegetarian, and would not be favoured in such an animal.

The dog possesses its characteristic, very specialised physical attributes because nature has favoured them over many thousands of years. It possesses its mental qualities for the

THE DOMESTICATED DOG

same reason. The dog is an alert, greedy, lusty, intelligent animal simply because those of its ancestors which possessed these qualities were the most successful in the struggle for survival.

It is easy to see the survival value to a dog of such mental qualities as alertness and intelligence. But what about traits like loyalty and responsiveness? Such qualities do not aid the success of an individual dog. Here the dog must be considered as a pack animal. The more loyalty the members of a dog pack showed to one another, the more successful that pack would have been. In fact a dog pack without loyal members would have had little success in such co-operative ventures as hunting and raising puppies. The successful dog pack produced more offspring than the unsuccessful one; and these offspring, of course, resembled their parents. Thus succeeding generations of dogs contained a progressively greater proportion of animals with the genetic make-up producing that quality which we call 'loyalty'.

Any discussion of canine mentality must include reference to those patterns of behaviour which we term 'instinctive'. At first sight it is easy to see overtones of rational behaviour in actions which are, in fact, purely instinctive. Thus it may seem rational for a terrier to kill a rat by shaking it and breaking its neck; indeed in its proper place instinctive behaviour does have rational consequences.

However, the terrier is not being rational; its behaviour is completely instinctive. The proof of this is that exactly the same behaviour can be stimulated in a situation where it is quite useless. The same terrier that shakes a rat to death will, with equal enthusiasm, shake slippers, shoes, sticks and toys. When Debbie catches a fly the unfortunate insect is accorded a similar battering, demonstrating clearly that when an animal acts instinctively it is quite ignorant of the effects of its action.

An even better example is to be found in the avian world. The common partridge escapes its predators by 'freezing'.

When it does so its brown colouring blends perfectly with the fields it frequents, rendering it almost invisible. At first sight one might imagine that the bird was behaving rationally; that it was using great cunning to evade its enemies. This view, however, is quite erroneous. Occasionally, by a freak of genetics, a partridge is born which is snow-white in colour. Yet when such a bird senses approaching danger it behaves in exactly the same way as its better camouflaged relations. It freezes! What more pointless action for a snow-white bird in a ploughed field? This proves conclusively that instincts are not based on reasoning but are simply stereotyped patterns of behaviour.

How, then, do these stereotyped behaviour patterns arise? The agency, once again, is the phenomenon of natural selection. Consider a bitch with her first litter of puppies. It is inherent in her nature to lick them clean after they are born. Such stereotyped behaviour was not, however, natural to primitive wild dogs. In this case different bitches had a greater or lesser tendency to throw a quick lick in the direction of their puppies, depending upon their genetic make-up. But those puppies which did receive a lick or two stood a greater chance of survival. They were cleaner and their breathing was not obstructed. So more puppies with mothers who licked them survived, than those with mothers who did not — and these puppies inherited, and passed on, the genetic fluke that made their mothers lick them in the first place.

Dogs, cats and other mammals that regularly return to the same sleeping-quarters usually keep those quarters very clean. They relieve themselves some distance away. The genetic make-up responsible for this inclination has survival value; it helps protect the animal from disease. For this reason cats and dogs are fairly easily house-trained, since the owner is merely reinforcing the animal's natural instinct. Yet it is virtually impossible to house-train a monkey because in nature, this animal does not return to fixed sleeping quarters. There is, consequently, no survival value for the instinct to be clean,

THE DOMESTICATED DOG

and it has not developed.

Natural selection comes into operation from the earliest days of a young animal's life. The strongest pup of a litter invariably wins the competition for the best feeding position, at one of its mother's hindmost teats. This is the best position for two reasons; firstly because these teats usually provide most milk, and secondly because they are snugly positioned between the mother's back legs. The remaining pups arrange themselves in decreasing order of strength and aggression, with the weakest finishing up at one of the front teats. This order is usually established by the time the pups are a week old. So even at this tender age, the strongest and most aggressive puppy stands the greatest chance of survival.

Recently, on the biological time-scale, natural selection has been interfered with by breeding or artificial selection. Unfortunately this has not always been for the best. Some breeders have concentrated on quite arbitrary points, forgetting how a real dog should look and behave. Often these fashionable excesses are deleterious to the dog's health. For example, certain miniature breeds have difficulty in carrying out many of their bodily functions, from respiration to reproduction.

Even so, the effects of artificial selection have been relatively small compared to those of natural selection. There are two reasons for this. Firstly, the period of time over which breeding has been used is infinitesimal compared to the thousands of years that natural selection has operated. Secondly, sensible breeding has often artificially selected in favour of qualities like intelligence, speed, loyalty, strength, and so on — the very features which natural selection itself has been developing!

I make no apologies for dwelling on the subject of genetics, as an animal's genetic make-up is the more important of the two factors which determine its personality. The other factor is the animal's environment — where it lives, who it lives with, how it is trained and so on.

THE DOMESTICATED DOG

Domestication

The domestication of the dog began about fifty thousand years ago. In comparison the cat, which was domesticated in ancient Egypt, is a relative newcomer. The modern dog's ancestors were prehistoric wild dogs; wolves, jackals and the like. As seen in Chapter 1 the majority of wild dogs are hunters and live in packs. There are exceptions, however. Some wild dogs are solitary animals while others scavenge in preference to hunting. It is very probable that the wild ancestors of the domestic dog were jackal-like scavengers. Fossil evidence indicates that prehistoric man first used the dog as a refuse-disposer. Archaeology has shown that he deposited his refuse, rotten meat, bones, pieces of skin and so on in piles a few yards from his living quarters and left it to rot. In hot weather this must have made a terrible smell as well as being a potential hazard to health. How many years did it take man to realise that the sly, stealthy jackals who came stealing from his evil-smelling piles were, in fact, doing him a service? Anyway, in a relatively short time a mutual tolerance must have grown up between early man and early dog. Probably a pack of canine retainers would attach itself to a group of stone-age men, never straying far from their settlement.

It must soon have become apparent to early man, that the dog was useful in another way: as a guardian against unwelcome intruders. At the approach of any large nocturnal predator the jackal-dogs would wake the settlement with their growling, and the stone-age men would rush to arm themselves and to stoke up the glowing embers of their fires. For the predator the element of surprise would have been lost. By this time mutual tolerance had flowered into mutual trust, so much so that certain of the dogs would accompany man on his hunting expeditions. Here the dog's speed and keen sense of smell must have been a tremendous asset. As a reward for their assistance in the hunt, a man would allow his dogs to devour the remains of the carcass. And as the partnership between man and dog became firmly established, so man must have introduced the dog into his dwelling-place. Perhaps an orphan puppy was the first animal to share his fireside. Now, at last, the dog was truly domesticated.

Selective Breeding

Once the dog had taken its place within the home, man started to breed his animals selectively and managed to evolve a strain more suited to its new mode of life, and which conformed more precisely to man's own requirements. Certainly the technique of selective breeding as we know it was at first practised unintentionally, yet the principle behind it is simple. Man selected those dogs which he liked, those that were strong, loyal, intelligent, gentle and so on, and bred from them. Many of the next generation of puppies therefore possessed the same desirable qualities, having inherited them from their parents. Likewise man discarded those dogs which were savage, nervous, sly and so on, ensuring that the next generation did not inherit their bad qualities.

This was probably man's first use of artificial selection and what a wonderful job he made of it! To appreciate this one has only to consider the dog's rather unsavoury ancestors. Compare the gentleness, loyalty and affection of today's animal with the savageness of the wolf and the sly cunning of the jackal. This healthy state of affairs persisted until the last century, with man regarding his dog as a workmate and a companion. Man's only concern was that the animals he bred were intelligent, good workers, and of a fine character. He would breed as often as possible from a dog possessing these qualities and as little as possible from one which did not. If nature presented him with a really bad dog, one which was physically malformed or mentally maladjusted he usually did the kindest thing for both the individual animal and the species in general: he shot it.

By careful breeding man was making his dog a really

magnificent creature. Then in 1859 a group of working-dog owners, rightly proud of their dogs' fine looks, organised the first dog show. A new criterion was introduced into breeding and henceforth some breeders concentrated on producing good looking dogs. I am very much in favour of breeding attractive dogs but think it essential that breeders should do their utmost to ensure firstly, that in addition to being good looking a dog possesses all the other fine canine qualities; and secondly, that the excesses of fashion do not result in the production of races of genetic freaks.

It should be obvious to any dog-lover that breeding for looks is valueless if done at the expense of the dog's character and intelligence. However, a few misguided breeders are willing to produce dogs of defective mentality provided that they win prizes at dog shows. The production and reproduction of temperamental and neurotic animals—particularly excessive inbreeding—has had deleterious effects on the species as a whole, often producing dogs which are very difficult to control. The solution to this problem is twofold. Firstly, breeders should make every effort to ensure that the puppies they produce combine good looks with a sound mind and a robust constitution. Secondly, every dog should be given a certain amount of good, intelligent training.

Turning to my second proviso for successful dog-breeding, very often breeders pay too much attention to what is fashionable rather than to what is good. Unfortunately fashion is a foolish and unpredictable mistress, yet even so the production of freaks persists. Every year dogs are bred with flatter faces, larger ears, shorter legs, more wrinkled noses, and curlier tails. Almost invariably these excesses are bad for the health of the dog in question.

I am fully in favour of breeding for looks provided that this does not involve sacrificing other, more important, features. As regards pedigree breeds, breeders have succeeded in the majority of cases in combining attractive features with fine intelligent minds. Alsatians, retrievers, Labradors, spaniels,

Dalmatians and the like are the noblest of animals. My concern is for the welfare of the minority of dogs that are bred for looks, and looks alone. To my mind this is a prostitution of our knowledge of the principles of genetics.

Selective breeding can strengthen or weaken an instinct but can never eradicate it completely. Neither can it implant a new foreign instinct into an animal. For example, I am sure there has never yet been a dog without some vestige of the hunting instinct — even if it only manifests itself in such substitute actions as chasing a ball or shaking a slipper. Yet however long artificial selection were employed it would not be possible to produce a dog with, say, the avian urge to incubate an egg.

Breeding can, however, divert or sublimate a dog's instincts. Most people would consider the herding instinct of a well bred working sheepdog to be far removed from the hunting instinct of a wolf; but this is not the case at all. The herding instinct derives from the occasions when a wolf pack was hunting a large animal, too powerful to be tackled by one or two wolves only. In successful packs the leading wolves, the strongest and fastest, would appreciate this and, instead of attacking the animal, would outflank it and herd it back into the path of their fellows.

Over thousands of years the careful breeding of working collies has diverted much of the hunting instinct of these dogs into the desire to herd. However, even now, a young or untrained sheepdog will sometimes rush in to 'grip' a sheep (and so will some old enough to know better!).

Some people express surprise that, in addition to sheep, collies will 'work' a wide variety of other animals. My Kim shows interest in cattle, ducks, horses, cats and even 'eyes' the deer in a local park. With an appreciation that the desire to herd devolves from the hunting instinct this becomes easier to explain. A sheepdog can be trained to herd any animal which, in nature, it would have hunted.

Before discussing the dog's instincts in more detail, I shall here touch upon the origins of the two main canine types.

THE DOMESTICATED DOG

Over the years man has used his dogs in a wide variety of capacities: from seeking out truffles (underground edible fungi) to guiding the blind; from drawing sledges to searching for lost mountaineers. Most modern breeds, however, are descended from dogs which have been bred to assist man in one or other of two principal functions: namely hunting and herding.

Let us first consider my own particular favourites, the herding dogs. The foremost of these, and the only type in universal use, is the working sheepdog or Border collie. These medium-sized dogs which originated around the border of England and Scotland are strong, fast, hardy creatures. They vary considerably in appearance. Their coats, commonly black and white, may encompass a wide range of colours; from chocolate to blue, from tan to grey. There is a similar variation in coat length. Some are short-coated, some are long-coated and the occasional 'beardie' is still to be seen.

Their one feature in common is their characteristic style of working sheep. They must not bark (unlike the Old English sheepdog) and they must not bite (unlike the Welsh corgi). For either of these two 'offences' a working sheepdog could be disqualified from a sheepdog trial. Instead a Border collie works by 'eye'. Half crouched, tail held low, it stalks slowly towards its sheep, fixing them with its stare. Closer and closer it approaches, its gaze never wavering till at last the sheep lose their nerve; they turn and move gently away. Rather than terrorise its sheep, a good working dog seems instead almost to hypnotise them.

Because Border collies may be observed in such a wide variety of shapes, sizes and colours, the uninitiated occasionally mistake them for mongrels. Nothing could be further from the truth. These dogs have been pure bred for their intelligence, character and working ability over thousands of years. By comparison many of today's pedigree breeds, few of which originated more than three hundred years ago, are relative newcomers: and some have yet to prove their worth.

Long term selection for good working dogs has produced a breed which is remarkably easy to train. They have a strong submissive instinct and are extremely eager to please. In recent years they have usurped the Alsatian as the most frequent winner of Cruft's obedience competitions. Their keenness to work is prodigal. At a sheepdog trial one often sees a line of black and white faces, brows furrowed with concentration, necks craned, observing the progress of their rivals' sheep. The working instinct is so strong that, on such an occasion, a bitch in season will snap at any dog which approaches.

Another advantage of the breed is the fact that it is not recognised by the Kennel Club. This has saved the Border collie from the fate of the corgi and the Old English sheepdog, both of which are having their working instinct bred out of them in favour of other, more arbitrary, features. Instead, the Border collie is recognised by the International Sheepdog Society. It is possible to acquire a registered sheepdog in two ways. Firstly if both parents are themselves registered, and are free from hereditary fault, and secondly on merit — if the dog wins a certain number of competitions. So with the Border collie, selection for character and intelligence continues; long may this be the case.

Hunting dogs comprise the other main canine group. The earliest hunting dogs probably bore a close resemblance to today's greyhound. In ancient Egyptian drawings slender, powerful dogs of this type are frequently depicted. The greyhound and its close relatives are, of course, exceptionally fast. Travelling in a straight line these dogs may reach speeds of up to forty miles an hour.

From greyhound-like ancestors other hounds were developed. These include foxhounds, elk-hounds, bassets, bloodhounds and beagles. All these dogs have dome-shaped heads, long ears, and, unlike the keen-sighted greyhound and its close relatives, hunt mainly by scent. Again unlike the greyhound, these more modern hounds 'give tongue' when hot on the trail of their quarry. The normal-sized hounds were too large to follow foxes, badgers and so on which 'went to ground' when cornered. So early in the development of the group a special type of small hunting dog was bred for the sole purpose of pursuing animals which took refuge down holes. Of necessity, these dogs were hardy, courageous animals and fierce, determined fighters. They were the progenitors of the modern terrier.

The instinct to hunt and fight still abounds in these excitable, quarrelsome, wiry-coated little dogs. For this reason they are often difficult to control. Similarly the urge to dig, instilled in them by years of selective breeding, is usually still prevalent. As a general rule the proud gardener would be well advised *not* to invest in a terrier! In the early nineteenth century terriers were used in 'ratting' competitions, a popular form of public entertainment. A good 'ratter' would kill one hundred rats in less than ten minutes. The record stands at one hundred rats in five and a half minutes.

In relatively recent times, today's gun dogs were, in the main, developed from the hound group. Spaniels, setters, retrievers and pointers all possess the long ears and keen sense of smell of the hounds. However, careful breeding has ensured that the gun dogs are calmer, steadier and of a gentler disposition than their ancestral type. They are also highly intelligent and easy to train.

One has only to watch a dog in a local park persistently returning a stick or ball to its weary owner to realise that retrieving is a natural canine instinct. The origin of this instinct, like that of so many others, can be deduced from a study of dogs in the wild. A rudimentary type of retrieving is performed by all those wild dogs which carry their prey home before devouring it; for example, the common red fox.

With gun dogs the instinct to fetch their prey home has been strengthened by selective breeding. The gun dog's hunting instinct has been diverted into the desire to retrieve, in just the same way that the hunting instinct of the Border collie has been transformed into the desire to herd.

A mature dog (or any other animal for that matter) may be compared to a photographic print. The success or otherwise of a photograph depends on two factors. Firstly the exposure, and secondly the development and printing. Bad printing can spoil even an excellent exposure, while good printing can make a bad exposure look presentable. To produce a really good photograph, both processes need to be well executed.

So it is with dogs. A genetically poor dog can be improved by careful training. A genetically sound animal can be ruined by inept training, or by no training at all. But a combination of a naturally excellent dog and careful, intelligent training is needed to produce a Cruft's obedience champion or a top-class working sheepdog.

3
CANINE BEHAVIOUR

Territorial rights

The drive for territorial ownership is common to all vertebrates — reptiles, amphibia, fish, birds and mammals. An animal that is successful in acquiring a piece of territory will drive off any intruder with the utmost ferocity. Such aggression is usually only directed towards members of the same species. Thus a grey squirrel, whose territory normally comprises either three large trees or five small ones, will attack any other squirrel which infringes its territorial boundaries. It will, however, happily share its property with birds, mice, lizards and so on.

It is very rare to find two male birds of the same species sharing a tree or hedge. Contrary to popular misconception male birds do not fight for their mates; their combats are entirely territorial. Territorial ownership has its advantages, however. The male bird possessing the largest, most imposing piece of real estate wins the heart of the best of the females. Analogous behaviour may be observed in the human species!

Here, then, is one advantage of territorial ownership. Other benefits are equally obvious. By winning itself an adequately sized portion of territory an animal is insuring against starvation. Territorial possession prevents overpopulation from depleting local food supplies. The members of a species become spread as widely as possible over the land area available to them. Territory is also an important factor in the struggle for existence between predators and their prey. A carnivore with a thorough knowledge of its hunting grounds

The Retrieve: *Plate 1 (above left)* Dumb-bell thrown, Kim awaits command: *Plate 2 (above right)* 'Fetch it'; *Plate 3 (below left)* The dog presents; *Plate 4 (below right)* Back to heel

Plate 5 Teaching Kim, the sheepdog, to stand

Plate 6 Heel, off the lead

stands the best chance of catching itself a tasty dinner. By the same token a small herbivore stands a better chance of dying of old age if it is familiar with every nook, cranny, shelter and sanctuary in its locality. Such knowledge is of particular value to the young of a species.

These two latter advantages of territorial ownership are also enjoyed by those groups of animals that jointly defend a tract of land. Man, like his simian ancestors, is both a social and a territorial animal. Throughout the ages territorial disputes have been a continual source of conflict between different human tribes and races. Man's aggressive territorial behaviour is equally prevalent in times of peace. Who would dare suggest to an ardent Liverpool supporter that Arsenal were a team of comparable ability, or extol the New York Yankees to a Detroit Tiger fan?

The semi-wild Eskimo husky dogs of Greenland divide themselves into groups of between six and twelve. Each group claims its own particular expanse of territory and very precise boundaries become established. These boundaries are known and recognised by every dog, with the sole exception of the immature males. These young animals continually violate territorial limits and, incidentally, suffer quite severe punishment for their efforts. This rough treatment appears to leave them completely unmoved. Immediately such a youngster attains sexual maturity, however, its whole outlook changes. No longer does it trespass on its neighbour's property and, indeed, it begins to co-operate in the defence of its own group's territory. Thus the dog's learning processes seem to be strongly reinforced by the animal's own natural development.

Certain animal groups including lion prides, wolf packs and antelope herds defend a territory which is in constant motion. It is not uncommon for a lion to fight to the death in defence of its perpetually changing territorial boundaries. The wolf's hunting territory is of particular interest. A wolf pack moves a few miles daily around the circumference of a circle about twenty miles in diameter. It only leaves the circle in order to make a kill. Each night the pack 'dens up' only to move on the following morning. So regular are the pack's movements that an experienced observer can predict to within a few hours its arrival at any point on the circle's circumference.

In its hunting territory the wolf is only mildly territorial, and the same is true of other wild dogs. The hunting territory of the Cape hunting dog frequently exceeds fifteen hundred square miles. This area will be shared by several packs and, obviously, no one pack could expect to defend an expanse of this magnitude. The dominant members of a pack of Cape hunting dogs occasionally 'mark' tree stumps and tufts of grass with their urine. This is more of a gesture, though, than a serious attempt to warn off rival packs. The jackal and coyote show a similar lack of possessiveness towards their hunting domain.

Wild dogs show a very different attitude towards their domestic territory; the area in which they court, mate and raise their young. As mentioned on p. 16, wolves are only pack animals for part of the year. Each spring the pack dissolves and individual pairs lay claim to a breeding area of about two or three acres. In this, their domestic territory, the wolves are intensely territorial. The male, sometimes assisted by the female, marks the boundaries with little squirts of urine. This is to warn off any casual passer-by; and woe betide any stray wolf that does violate the pair's boundaries. It will be driven off with the greatest ferocity. Jackals, coyotes and Cape hunting dogs show a similar jealous possessiveness towards their breeding grounds. The situation of the Cape hunting dog is slightly unusual in that the pack members stay together and jointly defend their domestic territory.

The domestic dog has inherited its ancestors' territorial instincts. In its hunting grounds, the local park, the high street and so on, the domestic animal shows little animosity towards strangers. Yet in its domestic territory, the boundaries of which coincide exactly with its master's garden fence, it is a different animal. It goes to considerable pains to ensure that every adjacent tree, lamp-post and fence is marked with its own peculiar trade mark. Frequently a dog that is amicable in the street will violently attack any stranger who dares penetrate its master's gate. A dog brought up in the home shows this guarding instinct much younger than one obtained from kennels.

Territorial animals are usually equipped with some sort of warning mechanism to scare off intruders. Many fish employ visual signals, frequently in the form of colour changes. Monkeys scream and chatter. The notion that songbirds sing for the joy of it is romantic nonsense. Their musical calls are an announcement of territorial ownership. Dogs, and many other mammals, mark the borders of their property with little squirts of urine — the smell of which is reinforced by the secretions of a special scent gland. It is a strange thought that a lark in song and a dog raising its leg to a lamp-post are both performing the same biological function.

A male dog is more preoccupied with territory than a bitch. So in order to spread his attentions as widely as possible a dog will urinate in little squirts. A bitch, however, normally empties her bladder in one go. It is for this reason that bitches are so damaging to lawns. Large concentrations of uric acid in one spot will kill even the hardiest of grasses. The only time that a bitch does not empty her bladder all at once is during and just before her season. At this time she distributes her urine as evenly as possible in order to inform every dog in the locality of her impending condition!

Aggression

Aggressive behaviour is closely linked to the phenomenon of dominance (see Chapters 1 and 4). A dog pack's social hierarchy is established and maintained by a combination of brute strength and aggressiveness. The acquisition and defence of territory is likewise very dependent upon deeds and displays of aggression. The interaction between territory and aggression is well illustrated by the stickleback. It is not difficult for an experienced observer to predict the outcome of a territorial dispute between two of these aggressive little fish. The stickleback which is nearer home is invariably victorious. The defeated fish will speed back deep into its own territory, hotly pursued by its conqueror. But as the loser approaches home his confidence returns; simultaneously his rival's aggression diminishes. A second encounter often ensues in which the roles of victor and vanquished are reversed. This process may be repeated several times, in a series of diminishing oscillations, until a precise boundary becomes established between the adjacent territories. As with the stickleback, the force of an animal's aggression is in direct proportion to its distance from home. It is for this reason that one may frequently observe a tiny dog energetically driving an animal of vastly superior size and power from its master's property.

Natural selection has favoured systems of territorial ownership — why? There are two great advantages to such a system. Firstly, it protects a species from overpopulation and possible starvation by ensuring that the members of that species are spread out as widely as possible. Secondly, a system of territorial ownership facilitates the operation of natural selection. The strongest, fittest, and most aggressive animals procure themselves the best available territory. Their chances of dying of starvation, thirst, or at the hands of a predator are thereby considerably reduced. These advantages are secured at the expense of their weaker, less fit fellows whose survival prospects are correspondingly worsened.

Aggression, therefore, is the means by which an animal realises its drives for both dominance and territorial ownership. It is a major biological instinct manifested by all animals — man included. There is a psychological school of thought which maintains that human aggression arises in response to frustration. Remove the frustrations from his life and man would become a peaceful animal. This theory may be quickly disposed of. Consider the United States or even Britain for that matter. The vast majority of the populace is well fed, well clothed and well housed; there is ample time for leisure, pleasure and permissiveness. But as these two countries become more affluent are they becoming more peaceful? The answer is an emphatic negative. In both Britain and the USA crime, violence and vandalism are increasing at an alarming rate. It is evident, therefore, that there is no correlation between human frustration and human aggression. What, then, is the root of man's aggression? In my view human aggressiveness stems from the fact that man is an animal, albeit a highly advanced one, and aggression is a characteristic feature of animal behaviour. This instinct has been favoured by natural selection over many millions of years. An instinct which has been developed so painstakingly cannot be expected to die out overnight. Aggression will be an important facet of the human personality for many thousands of years to come.

Hierarchical animals display a pattern of behaviour known as redirected aggression. A good example of this phenomenon is the pecking-order of farmyard chickens. If the top hen pecks its number two, this latter bird releases its anger by attacking hen number three, four or five. Similarly if the penultimate chicken is pecked by one of its superiors it will straightaway turn on the submissive little hen which is lowest in the social order. Likewise a wild pack dog that is bitten by a superior will often vent its fury by attacking a subordinate. Similar behaviour may be readily observed in a litter of domestic puppies. And how often does a man who has suffered a hard, tiring day at work return home only to take it out on his wife?

Display is a key factor in animal behaviour. Often a display of aggression is all that is necessary for an animal with territorial rights to dismiss an intruder. By the same method a dominant animal may exert his authority over a subordinate without resorting to physical violence. Display, then, is a mechanism for preventing damaging intraspecific conflicts. One only needs venture into a local park to observe a typical display of canine aggression. An aggressive dog stands erect, with ears pricked and tail held stiff and high. Its face wrinkles as it bares its teeth into an ugly snarl. As a result of all this the animal appears considerably larger and more ferocious than it really is. Simultaneously the hairs along the dog's spinal column become erect. This last action is hormonal and not under the animal's direct control. In cases of mild aggression the hairs erect themselves in about thirty seconds. But if the dog is fiercely aggressive more hormones are secreted and its hackles rise in five seconds or less.

The dog towards whom this aggressive display is directed may do one of two things. It may either acknowledge the first dog's dominance by adopting a submissive attitude, or it may call its rival's bluff and assume an equally aggressive posture. In the latter case the two dogs will make ever more threatening motions towards one another until one of them loses its nerve and hurriedly adopts the submissive position. Rarely are both dogs so confidently aggressive that a genuine fight ensues.

A dog's submissive display (see p. 10) is very characteristic. Often it will turn its head, exposing its throat to the dominant animal, thereby rendering itself completely vulnerable to attack. This cringing attitude has a pronounced effect upon the victor; having established his superiority his aggression melts away. Other animals, man included, have similar inhibitions about attacking a fellow when he is quite defenceless.

If one should encounter a large, strange, vicious-looking dog it is worth remembering that the animal is most likely putting on a display. In actual fact it is probably just as nervous as the person towards whom its threats are directed. In such a case the best course of action is to adopt a display of one's own, one of calm self-confidence. In the vast majority of cases the dog, its bluff having been called, will back away ferociously! This is not to say that one should attempt to become familiar with strange aggressive dogs. On the contrary one should aim to avoid them, or ignore them completely. The fatal mistake when encountering a strange dog, however, is to let the animal see that one is frightened of it. A dog is very sensitive to fear and a show of nervousness is liable to make it more aggressive than ever. It is a well known fact that those people who are manifestly terrified of dogs are the most likely to get bitten. It has often been observed that mad dogs do not attack drunks or very young children — persons who (for their own very different reasons) do not show any fear. One effect of fear on the human metabolism is to cause a slight sweating of the palms of the hands. This is quickly detected by a keen-nosed dog. So when one is introduced to a strange dog it is a good idea to close the fist and present the back of the hand for the animal's inspection. (This ploy has the added advantage that it makes it harder for the dog to amputate a finger!) An inexperienced dog handler often makes the mistake of keeping his charge on a very tight lead when in the presence of other dogs. His reason for so doing is a protective urge to draw his pet as far away as possible from any strange animal. A tight lead, however, transmits the handler's apprehensiveness to his dog and restricts the animal's movement, making it feel defenceless. In consequence the dog becomes frightened and snappy, and is therefore very likely to stimulate aggression in the soul of any strange dog which it may encounter.

Aggression is an intraspecific rather than an interspecific phenomenon. An animal will act aggressively towards others of the same, or a closely related, species. It will not, however, display aggression towards a member of a quite different species — even if this animal is its natural prey. Thus, in the presence of another member of the canine species, a dog will become a picture of aggression. It stands erect with teeth bared and hackles rising. Yet a dog that encounters, pursues and finally kills a rabbit will not at any stage display these characteristic aggressive gestures. A hunting animal bears its quarry no malice. Why, then, has natural selection decreed that only animals of the same kind should be aggressive towards one another? The answer is that a species is threatened more by its competitors, by those animals with the same vital interests, than it is by its predators.

If, for example, a certain type of hawk is suddenly protected by a conservationist law, then representatives of that species will become more abundant. The local mouse population, the hawk's prey, will suffer a corresponding decline. But if the number of mice is reduced too drastically there is no longer sufficient food to support all the hawks. So many birds, particularly the weaker ones, will die of starvation. A natural balance is established which keeps the ratio of mice to hawks at a fairly constant level. This balance also ensures that the mouse population is never completely eradicated by its avian predators. Although a species can never be wiped out by its predators it may suffer that fate at the hands of its competitors. An example of this is the manner in which a marsupial predator, now found only in Tasmania, was eradicated from the Australian mainland. Millions of years ago the marsupial wolf ranged throughout the entire Australian continent. Although a marsupial, this animal had the approximate form and structure of the mammalian dog: an interesting case of parallel development. At this time the true canine dog was unknown in Australia, so throughout its early evolutionary history the marsupial wolf suffered little serious competition. In a later prehistoric era the aborigines colonised Australia and with them they brought a primitive, semi-domesticated dog, the dingo. Many dingoes reverted to the wild state, hunting and scavenging in competition with the marsupial wolf. Though considerably more powerful than its canine rival the marsupial wolf was relatively slow and ponderous. Consequently the dingo encroached more and more into the marsupial wolf's food reserves, and finally the latter was wiped out from the Australian mainland. The species is now struggling for its evolutionary survival in Tasmania, an island outside the dingo's range.

The foregoing examples clearly demonstrate that a species is eradicated by its competitors rather than its predators. The behavioural phenomenon known as aggression is a natural device which ensures that competing animals are spread as widely as possible throughout their individual habitats. The survival of the maximum possible number of competitors is thereby ensured.

4
TRAINING, THE MAN/DOG RELATIONSHIP

Dominance

A dog may be trained to perform fairly complicated operations. It is difficult, though, to teach a cat to carry out even the simplest of tasks. This is common knowledge. However, few people appreciate *why* our two most popular pets are so different in this respect. Are cats less intelligent than dogs? Put this question to any cat owner (or to anybody who owns both animals) and the response is invariably an emphatic denial. I am in complete agreement.

To discover the reason for this anomaly it is necessary to consider the behaviour of each animal in the wild state. Both are carnivorous hunters, both are mammals and, in remote prehistoric times, both developed from a common ancestor. One of the major differences between the two animals is to be found in their social habits. Most wild cats are solitary creatures. They live and hunt either alone or in small family groups. In contrast most wild dogs are pack animals. A large number of dogs, only a few of which are related, live together as one unit.

As explained in Chapter 2, natural selection has favoured dog packs with firm leaders and loyal, obedient members. The most powerful dogs in each pack will display some form of leadership to a greater or lesser extent. Hence the wild dog, unlike the wild cat, does not make all his own decisions. Many important aspects of his life — his role in the hunt, his share of the kill, with which bitch he shall mate — are determined by his position on the pack's social scale. It is the natural instinct of a dog to accept and obey orders from an animal which he considers to be his superior. In contrast the wild cat does not live under the supervision of a pack leader, so all his actions are self-determined. The domestic cat has retained his ancestors' independence of spirit and refuses to take orders from anybody.

In consequence it is very difficult, if not impossible, to train a cat. A dog, however, is easily trained provided that the trainer is able to attract the obedience and respect that, in nature, the dog would offer to its pack leader. In other words the first task of an aspiring dog trainer is to convince his animal that he, the trainer, is master of their relationship. In a dog pack it is extremely rare for two dogs to share equal rank. This instinct has persisted in the domestic dog whose nature demands that he should separate all beings into two classes; his superiors and his subordinates.

An intelligent owner could not tolerate a situation in which he was dominated by his dog. But to share a relationship on equal terms is not in a dog's nature. It would find the circumstances confusing and disturbing, and might even turn vicious in an attempt to settle the issue. One alternative remains — for the trainer to dominate his dog. The type of domination I have in mind implies no unkindness. It simply means that in any day-to-day dispute, like whether a muddy dog is allowed on the furniture, the trainer gets his own way. The dog accepts this and does not argue the point.

How, then, does the dog trainer establish his dominance? He must adopt the method that the dog's pack leader would employ in nature; he must use force. It will be recalled from Chapter 1, however, that the system of hierarchical 'biting-order' is a very effective peace-keeping mechanism. Admittedly there is a certain amount of fighting amongst young dogs; but a hierarchy is rapidly established, and each dog knows which of his fellows he may threaten, and which he must appease — with the appropriate gestures.

Thus the best way that an owner can ensure a peaceful coexistence with his domestic dog is to assert his dominance from the very start. If possible it is best to train a dog from puppyhood. The young animal then accepts the trainer as its 'leader' at the same stage in its life as it would enter the 'biting-order' in the wild state. A happy peaceful relationship between man and dog will ensue.

The amount of force required to establish the trainer's dominance varies considerably from dog to dog; in general the larger breeds require more than the smaller ones. Some dogs are naturally more submissive than others, and there are some where a forceful manner may be all that is required. If so, so much the better. The intention should be to let the dog know who is boss with as little force as possible. Any sign of rebellion, like snapping, snarling, or baring the teeth, should be crushed instantly. The trainer must dominate his dog before the dog learns to dominate him! With a powerful dog like a great Dane or Dobermann it is even more important to establish firm control while the animal is young. The puppy must be taught that its handler can overpower it at will, and that he would be instantly victorious if any conflict should arise.

If the young dog can be suitably impressed with its handler's superior strength, this conviction will persist into maturity. By this means a young or small person can control a large, powerful dog. For example my wife Mary, not a large woman, maintains firm control over Debbie—a canine steamroller, with inch-long eye-teeth and a jaw that hinges through ninety degrees. Authority, once established, is, fortunately, seldom questioned.

A highly effective means of dominating a really difficult dog is to punish any misbehaviour by lifting it by the scruff of its neck and administering a firm shaking. To appreciate the effectiveness of this method it is again necessary to consider the dog in its wild state. Early in its life a wild dog becomes concerned with establishing its position in the pack's hierarchy. In the struggle for status it exchanges sharp bites with a number of its contemporaries. Thus it is in a dog's nature to expect a few hard knocks in the early months of its life. Consequently a wilful dog is not unduly impressed by any spanking which its long-suffering owner may dispense. A shaking, though, is a different thing. In the wild state it would take a canine Hercules, a veritable super-dog, to lift another clear of the ground and shake him. The miscreant dog is somewhat shocked and highly impressed by such treatment. This method is, of course, impossible with a truly vicious dog. Such problem dogs are often produced by the misguided 'spoiling' of puppies, which come to resent any form of discipline in later life. In most cases a little discipline early on would have produced a normal animal.

However, even a full-grown dog may be cured of its vicious streak. Such a redemption requires patience, and much more strictness than would have been necessary if training had commenced in puppyhood. A choke chain is essential to train a powerful, savage dog. It is the only practical means by which any opposition may be instantly overwhelmed.

At first sight shaking a dog by the scruff of its neck or jerking it on a choke chain seem rather violent methods of gaining control. It must be remembered, though, that a dog's neck is in no way comparable to the human organ. Even a superficial study of canine anatomy reveals just how well protected a dog is in this region. Dogs at play are continually biting one another's throats with no apparent ill effect.

Even so, a certain amount of discretion must be used in the application of these techniques. It would obviously be unkind to jerk the neck of a miniature breed with a chain like a battle-ship's anchor cable. It would be equally unkind to shake a dog, even a large one, which was of a very timid disposition. If a dog is correctly trained from puppyhood these strenuous and rather unpleasant methods will, almost invariably, be superfluous. It is much kinder to apply moderate correction to a young dog than be compelled to use violent correction (or have the animal put down) when it reaches maturity.

It is interesting to note that a dog always gives its loyalty to its trainer—to the person who dominates it. The fact that the animal may be fed by someone else has no bearing on the matter. Thus Kim is undoubtedly 'my' dog, although Mary feeds her more often than I do.

The instinct for hierarchical dominance and submissiveness is not confined to dogs, but is prevalent in every organised higher animal society. The German ethologist, Konrad Lorenz, has made a fascinating study of the very precise social order in jackdaw societies. The layman may make similar observations of 'pecking order' in chickens and a hierarchical 'butting order' in farmyard cattle.

Dominance is particularly marked in the primates. Members of a monkey tribe, like members of a dog pack, compete for their social position by biting one another. An equally good example arises in the behaviour of man himself. The instinct to dominate is the root of such human traits as snobbishness, class consciousness, acquisitiveness, the desire to 'keep up with the Jones's' and so on. Circumstances prevent a modern man from physically convincing other men of his superiority; he now has to resort to subtler methods. The term 'status symbol' means exactly what it says. It is a symbol of a man's wealth or ability, with which he hopes to convince his contemporaries of his superior social status. Rank plays a very important part in human behaviour. As well as the titled gentry, lords, earls, marquises, barons, dukes and the like, even the common man is very conscious of his place in society. He therefore regards himself as upper class or working class, as lower middle class or middle middle class, as a blue- or a white-collar worker.

Social hierarchy and its advantages have already been discussed in this and previous chapters, but it is nonetheless appropriate to emphasise the survival value of the system. Firstly the animals which adopt it are able to enjoy a harmonious, disciplined existence. In a dog pack such discipline is essential for the successful conduct of the hunt. Efficiency is also increased because the pack members do not waste time and energy fighting amongst themselves. The social order, once established, settles all arguments. Secondly, social order aids the survival of the strongest and fittest animals. The pecking-order of chicken is most pronounced at the feeding trough where the high-ranking hens command the best positions. In domestication, where all the hens are well fed, this is of little significance. However in the wild state, it would enable the high-ranking hens to survive times of famine, whereas those of lower rank would starve. That is to say, the strongest, fittest hens would survive at the expense of their weaker fellows.

Similar conclusions may be drawn from a study of the sex life of monkeys. Most monkeys are polygamous, with the males at the top of the social order mating with several females. At the other end of the scale, the rank of a few males does not permit them to mate at all. Hence the strong fit monkeys produce many offspring, which inherit the favourable genetic material of their parents, whilst the genes of the weaker monkeys are not passed on to future generations.

The above examples illustrate how social order increases the chance of survival of the strongest, fittest animals and also ensures that these same animals are the most prolific. In each case the success of the fittest animals is achieved at the expense of those which are less fit. So social order enables subsequent generations of a species to inherit the genetic material of the best animals of the previous generation. In other words, the reason that natural selection has favoured systems of hierarchical dominance and submissiveness is that these systems facilitate the efficient action of natural selection itself.

For a successful dog pack it is just as important that some members should be submissive as it is that some should be dominant, otherwise the situation of 'all chiefs and no indians' would prevail. The temperament of every dog, therefore, comprises a balance of the dominating and submissive instincts. In an individual dog these instincts may be present in roughly equal proportions, or one of them may be very strong at the expense of the other. Although some dogs possess only the slightest trace of the submissive instinct, there are very few in which it is completely lacking. Training of any sort develops a dog's submissive instinct and makes it more tractable for future exercises.

The greater a dog's submissive instinct, the easier it is to train. As mentioned in Chapter 2, the submissive instinct is very strong in dogs which, like the Border collie, have been bred for their working ability. A trained dog with a strong submissive instinct will obey its owner rather than yield to any conflicting desires of its own, like greed, curiosity, tiredness or lust. Kim will cheerfully come at my call even when eating her dinner. In contrast, Debbie is practically uncontrollable in the presence of food. Nothing gives a dog with a strong submissive instinct more pleasure than to please its master. At obedience classes the best working dogs invariably seem the happiest: they perform their tasks with keenness, alertness and a wagging tail.

Some dogs are considerably more difficult to train than others. Few, however, are impossible. Once a difficult dog is finally mastered it usually makes an excellent animal, courageous and full of initiative. Debbie has a poorly developed submissive instinct and is, therefore, quite difficult to train. She would rather please herself than please her owners. In the wild state a dog of her temperament would probably occupy quite a high position in its pack's social order.

A few patient (and courageous!) people have attempted to train wolves. In the case of wolf puppies their efforts have met with moderate success. These may be raised in a similar way to domestic pups, the main difference being their extreme shyness, their dislike of crossing open spaces, and their tendency to lurk in dark corners. If approached by strangers their fear may be sufficient to cause them to snap.

There have been several cases of wolf bitches remaining

Plate 7 Kim shedding: taking a single

Plate 8 Demonstrating the 'eye' of a Border collie

Plate 9 If the dog works well, praise it!

Plate 10 Debbie stands, showing the Dobermann's elegance

tame and obedient into adulthood. However, I do not know of any reported-case of a trainer maintaining his authority over a mature male wolf. A few have tried — usually with bloody consequences! The reason for their failure is the fact that the instinct for dominance is considerably stronger in the male wolf than it is in the female. Early in his life a young wolf dog experiences a powerful desire to attain the highest possible rank in his pack. The same thing happens in captivity. The young male wolf, though still friendly towards his trainer, eventually finds it imperative to settle the issue of dominance. Needless to say, the powerful-jawed wolf is always victorious.

Fortunately such encounters are rare with our domestic dog, which has had most of its ancestors' savageness and urge to dominate bred out of it. Even so, before any serious training can begin, the dog must be made to realize that the issue of dominance is settled — in its handler's favour!

Learning

Dogs and humans have many qualities in common — affection, expressiveness, greed, loyalty, laziness, jealousy, enthusiasm and intelligence, to name but a few. Because of this some dog owners assume that their pets possess *every* human quality, including morals, principles, the ability to reason, and so on. This quite incorrect attribution of human personality to animals is known as anthropomorphism.

The dog is an animal without morals and has no understanding of concepts like 'good' and 'evil'. Such concepts, of course, have no place in nature. They have been invented by, and for the benefit of, human society. Neither do dogs possess human-type intelligence. Primitive man was physically ill-equipped to compete with wolves, tigers and other large predators; the reason for his success was his vastly superior intelligence. Man learns by three methods: experience, reasoning, and communication (that is, by the written or spoken word).

It is impossible for a dog, having no understanding of the

human language, to learn by communication. It would be manifestly ludicrous carefully to explain to one's dog that, upon receipt of the command 'sit', it should stop in its tracks, bend its hind legs, straighten its fore legs, and lower its bottom to the ground.

Neither does a dog learn by reasoning, though this is sometimes disputed by those of anthropomorphic disposition. The scientific approach to any phenomenon is, however, to accept the simplest explanation; only when this is proved inadequate should a more complicated one be considered. Almost without exception canine learning can be explained in terms of experience, rather than by any powers of reasoning on the part of the dog. This is not to deny that some dogs are cleverer than others — the clever ones are either more susceptible to experience, or simply more experienced. Perhaps a couple of examples will illustrate my point.

One November afternoon I was training Kim in a large field of corn stubble. On this particular occasion the sheep were awkward, the wind biting and my temper short; even Kim seemed strangely out of touch. After about ten minutes I lost patience and shouted at Kim quite violently. Two days later I returned with Kim to the same field for her next training session. To my surprise she showed little of her usual keenness for work, and was reluctant to leave the vicinity of my car. Not wishing to upset her further I abandoned training and took her for a walk instead. During our walk we chanced upon another flock of sheep in a smaller, grassy field. At once Kim's enthusiasm returned: her ears pricked, her body stiffened and her eyes fastened on the sheep. Slowly she stalked them with the crouched, almost feline gait peculiar to a Border collie. Naturally I was delighted at her renewed keenness and, straightaway, gave her a short training session. Working in these quite different surroundings Kim scarcely put a foot wrong.

This example shows just how strong associations are for a dog. It also gives a clue to the working of the animal's mind.

Kim, quite incorrectly, associated the field of corn stubble with harsh criticism, and refused to work there again. She would, however, work perfectly well elsewhere. Had she possessed human-type powers of reasoning she would have appreciated that wherever I trained her there was a possibility that I might lose my temper. Had she been really logical she would have refused to work for me anywhere!

An even better example of the shortcomings of canine reasoning was witnessed by one of my friends. He was walking his spaniel through some woods when the pair encountered a particularly vicious bull terrier. A fight broke out between the two dogs, during which the spaniel was quite badly bitten. The incident made a lasting impression on the spaniel and even now, several years later, it refuses to go near the scene of the fight.

If such an attack had been perpetrated on a logical animal like a man, it would have affected him quite differently. Undoubtedly he would be reminded of the attack, by association of ideas, whenever he subsequently passed the spot where it occurred. However, a human intellect would grasp the true nature of the connection, and the man would feel no fear (unless, of course, he should once again run into the bull terrier!).

The mind of a dog works in a similar way to that of a very young child. A child of less than twelve months has not yet developed its faculty for logical thought; neither has it any comprehension of the media of communication. It learns purely by experience. It may, however, learn a great deal by this method. Thus a youngster has only to burn himself once, and he will avoid hot ovens for years afterwards. A dog learns by the same method. The canine mind has little grasp of the laws of cause and effect. It is a simple matter to teach one's dog to 'sit' at every kerb (by pushing its rump to the ground). It is, however, most unlikely that the animal will ever appreciate the *reason* for this ritual—namely the avoidance of road accidents.

The memory process by which a dog learns is termed 'association of ideas'. The principle is simple. Two stimuli are regularly applied to an animal in immediate succession. After a time the first stimulus, in addition to evoking its own response, will also trigger a response to the second stimulus, without the second stimulus being applied. Perhaps an example will make this clear. The Russian scientist Ivan Pavlov performed many pioneering experiments in the field of animal learning. In one such study he regularly preceded the feeding of his dogs (with a tasty meat extract) by the ringing of a bell. After several weeks he found that his dogs would salivate at the sound of the bell—even if no food were to follow. The response appropriate to the secondary stimulus (salivating) was triggered by the primary stimulus (sound of the bell) alone. The strongest associations, those things which are least easily forgotten, are caused by intense pain or pleasure. A child that has been burned is wary of hot ovens for years afterwards. Similarly once a dog has come to recognise its dinner bowl, there is never again the necessity to call it at meal time.

Another means of establishing a strong association is by constant repetition. Consider some examples of simple multiplication: 12×9, 9×7, 7×6. The average person will find that the answers fairly leap to mind. Yet his approach is neither logical nor mathematical; it is based on memory, and memory alone. In the vast majority of cases this knowledge was acquired by the constant repetition of multiplication tables in the person's childhood.

Having established that a dog learns by association of ideas, we can say that the secret of dog training is to ensure that any necessary associations become firmly implanted in the animal's mind. Here consistency is essential. Every time a dog behaves in the manner required of it, it should be treated to a very pleasant experience. It should be praised, fussed and petted out of all proportion to any cleverness it may have displayed. Likewise, every time it behaves undesirably a painful experience should be administered. With a sensitive dog harsh words may suffice; but with a tough, wilful creature a sharp cuff is occasionally needed. It is preferable to give a dog one nasty shock—promoting strong associations—rather than continual mild reprimands which the animal learns to disregard. Strong associations are established by continual repetition. Thus a well trained dog, like a well trained sportsman, needs regular practice. The average dog tends to lose its concentration after a few minutes; so five minutes training every day is considerably more beneficial than, say, fifteen minutes every three or four days.

There are two kinds of canine instruction. The first involves teaching a dog to carry out, on command, an action which is natural to it. The technique is very easy. Whenever the dog is seen performing the required action, the chosen word of command is repeated. After much practice the dog will come to associate the command with the action. Eventually it will carry out the action whenever the command is given—the natural desire is no longer required. It was by this method that, quite unintentionally, we taught Kim to roll on command. As a puppy she would often roll, sometimes to dry herself after a swim and sometimes just for the sheer pleasure of it. When we saw her we would encourage her and call 'roll over'. After a few months we found that she had learned to associate the words 'roll over' with the action. Nowadays we only need utter the words and she wriggles on to her back and waves her legs in the air.

The second type of canine instruction is used when teaching a dog to do something which is unnatural to it. The technique is slightly different, but again the principle is that of association of ideas. In this case the trainer pushes his dog into the required position in rather the same way as he would manipulate a puppet; simultaneously he repeats the chosen command. When a collie is working sheep its instinct is to crouch out of sight behind any available cover, like tall clumps of grass. The shepherd, however, wants the sheep to move, and they move much more readily if they can see the dog clearly. For this reason I decided to teach Kim to work standing up, something which was unnatural to her. When she crouched to 'eye' the sheep I would tell her to 'stand up'. At the same time I would lift her into the standing position with one hand beneath her belly and the other holding at the back of her neck. After a little practice she has come to associate the command with a hand raising her into the upright posture; she therefore rises to anticipate it.

Throughout this book I use the word 'command'. I do so for simplicity, but admit that in so doing I am indulging in anthropomorphism. The use of the word 'command' implies that the animal is conversant with the language in which the instruction is expressed. This is not the case. I employ the word to mean a call or sound that the animal has learned to associate with a particular action.

It is customary when pushing a dog into the sitting position to utter the word 'sit'. It would, however, be just as effective to use a word like 'oranges' or 'bananas' to establish the association in the dog's mind. Several years ago there was a music-hall act comprising a man and his dog. The dog was trained to perform, on command, various fairly straightforward tricks, but there was also a gimmick. When the trainer said 'stand up', the dog sat down; when he said 'sit down', it stood up; when he said 'go away', it approached him; when he said 'be quiet', it barked, and so on. The audience found this highly amusing and many of them thought it very clever. In actual fact it was no more, or no less, clever than teaching the dog to perform to more conventional commands. It should be obvious from the above that the actual words of command are quite immaterial. The only consideration is that they should be as brief and distinct as possible.

The most convenient and most widely used commands are those that are audible. A command may, however, impinge upon any one of the dog's five senses. Visual commands are very useful, particularly in such spheres as police work because they enable dog and handler to work together in complete silence. Their obvious disadvantage is that they are useless at night or whenever the dog is out of sight of its handler. Circus animals, like horses and elephants, are often trained to perform at the touch of a stick. It would be equally feasible—though rather impracticable—to train a dog by this method. Similarly there is no theoretical reason why the dog's senses of taste and smell should not be used as the receptors of commands.

Because canine learning is so dependent upon the principle of association of ideas, the dog will readily pick up unwanted associations. In the obedience exercise 'stay and recall' such an error is frequently seen. Correctly executed the exercise is as follows. The handler sits his dog down, tells it to 'stay', and walks to the opposite end of the room. He turns to face his dog, pauses, and then calls it to him. On receipt of the command 'come here' the dog returns to its handler.

The most common fault in this exercise is for the dog to return to its handler immediately he stops and turns to face it, without waiting for the recall. This error is caused by poor training. The inexperienced handler allows an unwanted association to develop in his dog's mind by always recalling the animal as soon as he faces it. An intelligent dog quickly learns to anticipate the recall. This fault may be remedied by preventing the unwanted association from developing. After turning, the experienced handler will always pause a few seconds before summoning his dog. No association develops because the turn and the recall are separated in time.

5
THE PRIMARY AIDS

Encouragement and Correction

To some of my readers the notion of disciplining their dogs may seem rather repugnant. However, there are two reasons why I consider a reasonable amount of correction both justified and desirable. Firstly, in my experience, well disciplined dogs are always happy dogs. Spoiled dogs, like spoiled children, are invariably fat, sullen and snappy. The dog is a highly intelligent animal, and for its general well-being it requires mental, as well as physical, exercise. Additionally a well trained dog gains tremendous satisfaction from pleasing its handler. This stems from the fact that the majority of our dogs' ancestors were pack animals. An efficient pack required firm leaders and loyal obedient members. For this reason natural selection operated in favour of those pack dogs who enjoyed obeying their leaders. A well disciplined domestic dog obtains similar pleasure from obeying its trainer. Thus the skilful handler uses his dog's submissive instinct for both his own, and the animal's mutual satisfaction.

The second reason for my belief in discipline derives from man's early association with the dog. When man domesticated the dog, he did so largely for his own benefit. The early semi-domesticated animal made a wonderful guard and its speed and keen nose made it a welcome hunting companion. In exchange man gave his dog a secure home, food, shelter and a fire to warm itself by. Thus from the beginning, man's relationship with the dog was one of symbiosis; that is, to the benefit of man and dog alike. It is only recently that man has allowed to develop the type of pet dog which accepts all that it is offered, but which gives little or nothing in return. This kind of relationship borders on parasitism — with man in the role of host! I believe the former approach to be far healthier. A dog is happier if it is permitted to contribute something, if only its respect and obedience, to the alliance. However, even respect and obedience do not appear automatically. They have to be fostered by man's kind, fair and firm treatment of his charge.

The whole idea of training is to encourage the dog to pursue those of its instinctive activities which are desirable to the trainer, and to deter it from those which are undesirable. Once again the principle of association of ideas is used. Those things which the trainer wants his dog to do must be made to seem agreeable to it; and similarly, those things he does not want it to do must be made disagreeable. For example consider a fairly common undesirable canine habit; that of chasing cyclists. The reason that a dog enjoys chasing cyclists, cars, and so on is that anything moving appeals to the animal's hunting instinct. Rarely does the dog bear any animosity towards the cyclist, and if the latter dismounts and stands still the dog quickly loses interest.

To break a dog of this habit it is necessary to create, in the animal's mind, an association between cyclist-chasing and an unpleasant experience. This may be achieved by persuading a co-operative friend to cycle past the house, bearing a rolled-up newspaper. The dog is given complete freedom to commence the chase. But when the dog is almost upon him the cyclist should dismount and attack it with his newspaper. Simultaneously he should shout loudly and fiercely, so as to give the dog the fright of its life. The idea of using a rolled-up newspaper is that it achieves maximum noise with minimum damage — the greater the fright, the stronger and more permanent will be the association. With any luck the next time a cyclist passes, the dog will steer well clear of him; this technique is particularly effective with a young and impressionable dog.

THE PRIMARY AIDS

In the same way, whenever a dog successfully accomplishes one of its exercises a tremendous fuss should be made of it. Affection, so long as it is not taken to ridiculous extremes, is in no way bad for a dog. Quite the reverse; it bolsters the animal's confidence and helps to cement the relationship between man and dog.

It is worth noting here that whether a dog's behaviour is desirable or undesirable is entirely dependent upon the needs of its trainer. If my sheepdog were to bark when working I would be very disappointed in her. On the other hand, the trainer of a guard dog would be equally dismayed if his charge did *not* bark when carrying out its duties.

The words 'reward' and 'punishment' may be defined as retribution for good and evil respectively. A dog, however, knows neither good nor evil, thus the use of these words is anthropomorphic; for example, it is ludicrous to suggest that a dog is being 'good' when it drives an intruder from its master's property, and 'bad' when it kills a rabbit—in both cases the animal is simply following its instincts. For this reason the terms 'encouragement' and 'correction' are preferable. There are three important considerations when encouraging or correcting a dog. Firstly, the encouragement or correction should be immediate; secondly it should be consistent; and thirdly the dog must *understand* what association the trainer is trying to establish in its mind.

The reason that correction (or encouragement) should be immediate will be obvious to anyone whose method of training is based upon the principle of association of ideas. Unfortunately all too few people use this method—or any method at all, for that matter! How often does one see dog owners attempting to cure their animals from running away by punishing them on their return? This causes the dog to associate returning to its owner with an unpleasant experience. Hence the dog is not dissuaded from running away but merely discouraged from returning after it has run away! How, then, does one secure the speedy return of a truant dog? The answer is to make the dog

THE PRIMARY AIDS

feel lonely and unprotected, so that it craves the security of human company. A lost dog, particularly a lost puppy, quickly loses its self-confidence. Next time your dog refuses to come when you call do not be tempted to chase after it because, apart from being somewhat undignified, this is playing into the animal's hands. Most dogs thoroughly enjoy a good chase. Instead try sneaking off and hiding behind a tree or a hedge. In a few minutes your dog will miss you and, in most cases, it will show signs of alarm. It may start searching for you, or perhaps it will sit down and whine nervously to itself. Do not reveal yourself at this stage; if you do the dog will probably resume its disobedience. Stay hidden a few minutes longer and let the dog really 'sweat it out'. Now is the moment to reappear, and when you do so the dog will usually display its relief by bounding joyfully towards you. As it approaches keep repeating the command 'come here' so that it associates the words with the action. When it arrives give it plenty of praise and fussing, and perhaps a biscuit or two. Make obedience seem a highly agreeable course of action. If your dog is an insensitive brute that feels not the slightest tremor of uncertainty when left to its own devices this method will, obviously, be unsuccessful. In a later chapter I will suggest other ways of making a more difficult dog seek the security of your company.

It should be obvious from the above that to 'punish' a dog by not feeding it, by omitting its daily walk or by keeping it chained outside is of no educational value whatsoever. In fact this type of correction is literally worse than useless because it may derange the animal and make it vicious.

Correction should be consistent. If a dog is always scolded and thrown off the furniture, it will quickly learn that its place is on the floor. If, however, it is allowed on the furniture when it is clean but ejected when muddy it will be confused by the inconsistency (a dog cannot appreciate that dirty paws spoil chairs). As well as making for a confused dog, inconsistent discipline also makes for a sly one — the type of animal that always 'tries it on' in the hope of getting away with it. A sad example of inconsistent discipline is when an owner allows his dog to chew his old slippers, but gets angry when it chews his new ones as well. What does he expect? Subtleties like the age of footwear are beyond the grasp of a dog's intellect. So far as chewing goes, the safest thing is to allow a dog to chew his toys, his bones, and nothing else at all.

Finally, it is essential that the dog understands the associations that the handler is trying to implant in its mind. For example, when Kim was younger she would occasionally bite a sheep. Whenever she did so I threw something at her and shouted angrily; she quickly learned to associate sheep biting with an unpleasant experience, and has given no trouble since. This fault was easily remedied, but others have proved much more difficult. One such problem was Kim's tendency to run too close to her sheep when I sent her to fetch them (on a correct 'cast' the sheepdog skirts its sheep as widely as possible until it arrives at their rear). In this case to discipline her would have served no purpose. She would not have understood the reason for my displeasure and might even have come to associate working itself with an unpleasant experience. Fortunately I am blessed with a patient and understanding wife, and it was with her assistance that I was able to solve this problem. When I practised casting Mary would position herself between Kim and the sheep and would, with much running and arm waving, shoo her out on to a correct course.

Before disciplining a dog it is essential to decide whether the animal is being disobedient, or whether it simply does not understand what is required of it. In the latter case correction is quite useless — it will merely destroy the dog's confidence. In cases of uncertainty the dog should always be given the benefit of the doubt. If after much practice the dog still does not appreciate what is wanted, it is up to the trainer to change his approach. Sometimes he may have to vary his approach several times before achieving the desired result. All this requires considerable agility of mind, intelligence and

THE PRIMARY AIDS

patience on the part of the trainer.

The trainer should regard encouragement as his primary teaching aid. Sometimes, though, encouragement alone will not be sufficient to teach a dog a particular exercise. It is at this stage that compulsion becomes necessary. Compulsion often has to be used to teach a dog something which is unnatural to it. For example, when teaching a dog to retrieve, it is usually a simple matter to persuade the animal to pursue and take hold of its dumb-bell because this part of the exercise evokes the powerful hunting instinct. It is doing what comes very naturally to it. The difficulties usually arise when one endeavours to persuade the dog to return with the dumb-bell, that is to utilise its less strongly developed retrieving instinct, and then to part with its artificial quarry. This part of the exercise often requires a degree of compulsion for its successful accomplishment. If the dog refuses to return with the dumb-bell the exercise should be repeated using a choke chain and lead. A few sharp jerks and the animal quickly realises what is required of it. If the dog will not let go of the dumb-bell, sharp words followed, if necessary, by a light tap on the nose usually do the trick.

Although a gentle-natured dog, our Dobermann is very strong-willed and stubborn. Consequently her training has involved the use of a considerable amount of discipline. But without firm handling a dog with her power would be a menace, capable of inflicting severe damage upon person and property alike. Our sheepdog is a very different sort of dog. She always does her utmost to please, whereas Debbie seeks only to please herself. This makes Kim a very easy dog to train and she is at her best when praise is lavished upon her. Unlike Debbie, Kim is very sensitive to criticism which upsets her and undermines her confidence. Thus individual dogs require widely differing amounts of discipline to bring out the best in them, and it is up to the handler to decide just how much correction is suitable for his dog. This decision requires considerable patience, observation, judgement and good sense.

THE PRIMARY AIDS

Although Debbie is more difficult to train than Kim, it does not follow that she is any less intelligent. All dogs have the same basic instincts, but they possess them in different proportions. In Kim's case, as with most working dogs, the submissive instinct has been bred for (see Chapters 2 and 4) and is very strong, so strong that it over-rides her other, more troublesome, instincts. In Debbie's case natural drives like greed, the urge to hunt and so on frequently overwhelm her less strongly developed submissive instinct. So although she probably understands just as many commands as Kim, it is much harder to secure her obedience.

As explained earlier, it is very important that a dog's correction should be immediate. When training Debbie not to worry sheep we would go to considerable pains to catch her red-handed. My wife would exercise her at the far end of a field containing three or four rams. Meanwhile I would sneak off and hide behind a tree in close proximity to the rams. When I had concealed myself Mary would walk with Debbie towards the rams. When the Dobermann spotted the rams her instincts invariably got the better of her and she would rush towards them bubbling with evil intentions. When she was almost upon them I would leap out from behind the tree and hurl my stick at her with a shout of rage. At this Debbie would freeze in her tracks and then scuttle back to Mary as fast as her legs would carry her. She has now come to associate sheep-chasing with unpleasant consequences and is usually able to control herself.

It is very useful if you can catch your dog in the act of thinking about misbehaving. This is quite easily done because most dogs are very expressive creatures — Nature has not yet selected for a 'poker-faced' dog! As I have mentioned before, when Kim was a puppy she would occasionally bite a sheep, something I could easily anticipate because instead of carrying her tail low, as when working correctly, she would rush in with her tail up. A few sharp words at this juncture would usually deter her before any damage was done. So if you see your dog about to purloin the Sunday joint, do not hesitate to clip his ear. Smack him for even thinking about it! The smack would, of course, be unjustified if one's training were based on the anthropomorphic concept of 'punishing' the dog for doing 'wrong'. This type of correction is highly effective, however, because it fully utilises the concept of association of ideas. The dog will come to associate thinking about taking the meat with an unpleasant experience. Next time, with luck, he will not even consider it.

Having discussed when to discipline a dog it now remains to consider the method of correction. The best possible way is to allow events themselves to form their own punishment. The advantage here is that the dog comes to associate its actions with unpleasant consequences but does not become frightened of its handler. When we first bought our Dobermann she was forever chewing her basket. To her the woody flavour and crunchy consistency was almost irresistible. At this stage she was a newcomer to our family and we did not want to lose her confidence. Our problem, then, was to make basket-chewing unpleasant without displaying any animosity towards her. Our solution was to apply a mixture of mustard and pepper to the more tempting parts of her basket. Soon she came to associate basket-chewing with a stinging tongue. The results of her actions were disagreeable to her, and she stopped. Unfortunately not all of our disputes with the strong-minded Dobermann have proceeded so swiftly to such a satisfactory conclusion.

This indirect method of disciplining a dog is very effective. On occasions, however, it is necessary to apply the correction personally. One reason for so doing is that the above method is often rather laborious and time consuming; another reason is that it is necessary for the handler to establish his dominance over the dog (the issue of dominance was discussed at some length in Chapter 4). If a Pekinese or a chihuahua were to throw its weight about one would scarcely notice. But if a large, powerful dog like an Alsatian or a Dobermann were to run wild it could cause serious damage. In such cases the unfortunate animal is often put down. How much simpler and kinder if the handler had exerted his authority from the very start!

Some dogs require much more correction than others. A strong-willed dog is usually difficult to train and requires considerable discipline. Perseverance is worthwhile, however, because such animals often develop into fine dogs—loyal, courageous, and full of initiative. On the other hand the confidence of a more submissive dog may be sapped by over-correction. It is also necessary to treat a puppy with considerable leniency, in the same way as one would treat a very young child. When correction becomes essential a sharp word will usually suffice. With a tough wilful dog a hiding with a rolled-up newspaper is often very effective—the newspaper causes the dog no harm but makes a frighteningly loud noise. Even so the blows should be applied to the animal's rump and not to a sensitive area like the end of its nose. I have heard it said that such treatment makes a dog hand-shy. In our experience this is not the case. Rarely does a week pass by without our unruly Dobermann being corrected, sometimes quite severely, for her misbehaviour, yet she shows not the slightest sign of hand-shyness. She loves to be petted and enters into a romp with good-natured enthusiasm. Our tone of voice and bearing towards her leave her in no doubt as to when she is being corrected and when we are simply playing with her.

When it becomes necessary to be really severe with a dog a good method is to shake it firmly by the scruff of the neck. As well as being physically uncomfortable such treatment makes a lasting impression on the animal's nervous system; for this reason it should never be used with a puppy or a dog of nervous disposition. It is, however, very useful with a powerful stubborn animal.

The best and most effective means of encouragement and correction at our disposal is that of 'secondary association'. When one of our dogs pleases us we make a terrific fuss of the

Stay and Recall: *Plate 11 (above left)* 'Stay'; *Plate 12 (above right)* The hesitation, to ensure the dog does not anticipate her recall; *Plate 13 (below right)* 'Come here'

The slip-collar: *Plate 14* Incorrect application, tightened by weight of lead
Plate 15 Correct application, slackened by weight of lead

THE PRIMARY AIDS

animal and perhaps give it a titbit to eat. At the same time we voice our pleasure by repeating 'good girl' (or a similar expression of praise) in very warm tones. Eventually an association develops in the dog's mind between our pleasure and the words 'good girl'. In other words the dog comes to regard the words themselves as a pleasant experience, so that a physical reward is no longer necessary. To demonstrate the effectiveness of this secondary association we have only to say 'good girl' to our dogs; at the sound of these two words Kim's tail and Debbie's stump start to wag happily.

Similarly, if we have to discipline one of our dogs the correction is always accompanied by a scolding in harsh tones. By now they have both come to associate expressions like 'bad dog' with physical punishment — and very often the words alone are all the correction that is required; a harsh tone of voice is sufficient to cause Kim's tail to flatten along her belly and Debbie (who does not possess a tail worth mentioning) to shiver with fright. The use of secondary association has two obvious advantages. Firstly it allows the dispensation of punishment without physical violence, and secondly it facilitates correction and encouragement when the dog is out of its owner's reach.

To build up these secondary associations it is important that one should be very communicative towards the dog. When correcting a dog put a snarl into your voice. When pleased, praise it with real enthusiasm; make certain it feels sure that you are delighted with it. People who talk to their dogs and are expressive towards them usually make good trainers. Finally, remember to change from encouragement to correction, and vice versa, immediately the dog alters its behaviour. If your dog is disobedient, scold it. But as soon as it stops misbehaving change your voice to one which is full of praise. This technique makes best use of the principle of association of ideas, the method by which a dog learns.

6
ELEMENTARY TRAINING

The average person should find it quite easy to train a normal, moderately submissive dog to behave itself around the house. If the owner has some idea of the workings of the canine mind his task will be considerably simplified. Occasionally, however, an owner will find himself in possession of a dog which he is unable to manage. If so, he (or she) has four alternatives: to get rid of the dog; to accept the chaos; to send the dog to a trainer; or to take his unruly pet to obedience classes.

The first two alternatives are defeatist and will be unacceptable to any peace-loving dog-lover. Despatching the offending animal to a skilled trainer may appear a highly attractive course of action. It has one great disadvantage, though. In most cases a fortnight with a skilful, experienced trainer will render the dog a more tractable, more obedient animal. The problems arise after it has been home for a week or so. Being a very perceptive animal, the dog soon realises that, while it was necessary to obey a professional, it can still lead its inexperienced owner a miserable life.

One alternative remains: for dog and handler together to attend a local obedience class. Such classes are both educational and entertaining and cost only a few pence per attendance. One is able to observe a wide variety of breeds obeying and disobeying their owners. After about a dozen lessons the average dog will know and respond to the commands 'sit', 'stay', 'heel', 'leave', 'come here', and 'be quiet'. The owner may be content with this and discontinue attendance. On the other hand he may decide to attend further classes where the

ELEMENTARY TRAINING

dog will learn more advanced exercises like retrieving, recall, and scent identification. If the dog shows sufficient ability and enthusiasm the pair may eventually be inspired to enter obedience competitions. If dog and handler attend classes once a week it will also be necessary to devote five or ten minutes a day to practice. As stressed in Chapter 4, the dog's daily training should never exceed ten minutes; if one attempts to teach too much, too quickly the animal will soon lose interest and concentration.

It is worth mentioning that even in elementary obedience classes one sees relatively few problem dogs. Far more commonplace are problem owners; people to whom dog training does not come naturally. At obedience classes such handlers are instructed in the techniques of dog training and are able to master their shortcomings. Problem owners often fall into one (or both) of two categories—those that are too quiet with their dogs, and those that are too lax. The former have trouble 'getting through' to their dogs and leave the animals uncertain as to how they should behave. To overcome this problem a conscious effort must be made to praise and criticise the dog loudly, clearly and emphatically. Those who are lax are asking for trouble. A spoiled dog is a sullen, snappy unpleasant creature. Dogs, like children, require and respect a reasonable amount of discipline. Anyone who thinks otherwise should attend an obedience competition, where they will straightaway be impressed by the cheerful manner of the participants. The sight of so many wagging tails will quickly dispel any doubts regarding the value of discipline.

Every time a dog obeys a command its education takes a step forward. Every time it disobeys, or fails to obey, its education takes a step back. For this reason it is quite pointless for a handler to give a command that he knows will be disregarded. It is better that the dog's training should fail to progress than that it should take a retrograde step. By the same token a dog should be compelled to carry out any command, however unimportant, that has been addressed to it. Outsiders can be a nuisance in this context. They often give one's dog a command in a half-hearted tone to which the animal hesitates to respond. If the animal disobeys they will happily accept the situation rather than compelling its compliance. They do not appreciate that in so doing they may be nullifying the effects of weeks of careful training.

It must be remembered, though, that no amount of firmness or severity will have any effect upon a dog that does not understand what is required of it. It is both morally and educationally objectionable to punish a dog that is doing its utmost to please a handler who cannot make himself understood. It is here that flexibility is very important. If a dog seems to be making very little progress with a certain exercise it is up to the trainer to change his approach. Canine perception varies considerably. A dog will quickly grasp one training technique, yet find a second technique quite unintelligible. Another dog, of similar intelligence, will respond to the latter method, but find the former completely confusing. For this reason two or three different approaches to each of the more advanced exercises will be suggested. As emphasised in my Preface, the handler should pick the method that he thinks will best suit his own dog. If the selected method proves ineffective the handler should abandon it and attempt another. Sometimes a combination or alternation of several techniques will prove the most beneficial. If the dog still fails to show a glimmer of understanding it is up to the handler to invent a technique of his own, one that he feels will suit the temperament of his particular dog.

The trainer's first task is to teach his pet to behave itself around the house, and the sooner training commences the better. Even a ten-week-old puppy will benefit from two or three minutes a day of patient instruction. First of all the dog must be house-trained. This is usually a fairly straightforward process, as all animals born in a nest show an instinctive desire to keep their living-quarters scrupulously clean. As soon as a fox cub is old enough it will leave the den to relieve itself.

ELEMENTARY TRAINING

Given the opportunity a domestic puppy will behave in a similar fashion. Yet if the same puppy were housed in a filthy kennel its urge for cleanliness would quickly disappear. Thus the first rule of house-training is simply to allow the dog to follow its own natural instincts. After every meal or drink the animal should be put out into the garden for five minutes. With a young puppy considerable leniency should be exercised. When it cannot be supervised it should be left in an old room with newspapers covering the floor. When the puppy does make a mess it will instinctively use the same spot — commonly a corner of the room. The next stage is to remove all the newspapers from the floor except those in this one corner. After a couple of weeks the puppy will realise that it may only relieve itself on the newspapers. Once this fact is firmly implanted in the animal's mind the newspapers may be moved, towards the back door at first and finally out into the garden (or wherever the owner desires his pet to perform its toilet). When the dog understands what is required of it, and is old enough to have more control over its body, the handler can take a firmer line. Whenever the animal disgraces itself he should address it in severe tones and despatch it roughly into the garden.

We have successfully taught our two bitches to empty their bladders on command. This is very useful last thing at night, before visiting friends, or prior to a long car ride. We simply take them into the garden or on to some waste-land and tell them to 'be good girls'. So eager to please is Kim that she will crouch obediently even when her bladder is quite empty. It is obvious to us when she is cheating though, because her tail is anxiously flattened along her belly. Impossible! To teach a dog to do this is much simpler than one might imagine. The technique relies on the principle of association of ideas. Whenever a dog is seen performing its toilet the handler should repeat 'be a good girl' or a similar expression of enthusiasm, depending on the sex of the dog and the taste of the handler. After a lot of practice an association forms in the dog's brain between the words and the action. Eventually the words alone are adequate to stimulate the animal's urinary system.

As early on in life as possible a puppy should be taught to come to its owner's call. Every meal-time presents the handler with a golden opportunity to practise this exercise. The puppy is taught to associate obedience with a very pleasant experience — its dinner! Regrettably this simple technique is not always a complete success. A clever dog quickly learns to anticipate the time and place of its feeding. Call it at mealtime and it arrives in a second. But try repeating the exercise when it has eaten its dinner! In such a case the handler must resort to other methods.

During the ensuing battle of wits the handler must exercise great self-control. Few things are more annoying than a dog that will not come when it is called. Yet the angrier the handler becomes the less inclined will the dog be to rejoin him. As said in Chapter 5, a handler will not cure his dog of running away by disciplining the animal on its return — such treatment will merely render the dog less willing to return on subsequent occasions. It is important that the handler should praise his dog, through clenched teeth if need be, when it does at last respond to his call.

There are, however, several stratagems by which an owner may secure the speedy return of his miscreant pet. The simplest of these is an extension of the 'meal time' technique. The handler carries in his pockets a number of biscuits or sweets which are used to reward the dog when it answers his call. When the dog has mastered the exercise the use of such titbits may be progressively abandoned. The technique of hiding from the dog to destroy its self-confidence, discussed in Chapter 5, is often successful with a young or sensitive animal. Unfortunately, though, this approach makes no impression upon a tough, wilful, self-confident dog. The problem here is that the dog is so self-assured that it has no qualms about being deserted. In a case like this the following technique is sometimes effective. The handler sets out for a training session carrying with him a small can, a coffee tin perhaps, half filled with stones. When the dog refuses to return the handler surreptitiously lobs the can of stones in its direction. The dog is startled by the sudden noise and feels a need for the protection of its master's company. It is most important that the dog does not perceive the origin of the can of stones. If the animal notices its handler throw the can the exercise has precisely the opposite effect to that intended — it will become nervous of its handler and be even more reluctant to return. A word of caution. This method should only be employed with a dog that is tough, resilient and assured. Its use with a dog that is young, sensitive or timid is liable to distress the animal and to destroy its self-confidence.

Yet another method is to take the dog into an open space with about twenty foot of light cord attached to its collar. The handler holds the other end of the cord and manoeuvres himself so as to keep it slack. This gives the dog the impression that it is running free. Periodically the handler should call his dog. If it obeys it should be praised profusely. If the dog ignores his call the handler should gently take up the slack in the cord. He should then repeat the command in a firm tone and simultaneously give the cord a sudden, sharp jerk pulling the dog towards him.

Four useful commands may be quite simply taught. The first of these is the word 'no' — used when the dog is doing, or thinking about doing something forbidden to it. If, for example, the handler notices his dog chewing the sitting room carpet he should say 'no' in a loud, harsh voice. Sometimes the fierce tone will be sufficient to deter the dog. If so it is learning the meaning of the command. If, however, the animal continues chewing it should be pulled quite roughly away from the spot. Simultaneously the word 'no' should be uttered in even fiercer tones. With a little practice the dog will appreciate the meaning of the word. At this stage fierce tones and rough handling become unnecessary. So well does Kim understand the word that I can use it in an almost conversational sense. When out walking she loves to bound ahead of me. If this causes her to follow the wrong fork of a path I need only call out 'no Kim' and she retraces her steps to take the correct turning.

A dog that jumps up is a nuisance. It dirties clothes and ladders nylons. It is also likely to frighten people who are not used to dogs, particularly children. In this case prevention is better than cure. A young puppy that jumps up should be told to 'get down' and gently pushed to the ground. A St Bernard puppy that jumps up may be quite harmless and very appealing. But if this habit is encouraged and allowed to persist into adulthood the dog will become an absolute pest. Yet who could condemn the animal for wanting to show its affection? The blame lies with the owner — for his lack of anticipation. To cure a mature dog of this habit requires considerable firmness. The animal should be told to 'get down' and knocked to the ground quite roughly. Even this treatment will not deter a really enthusiastic jumper, the sort of dog that leaps at one from ten feet away. To dampen the enthusiasm of such an animal the handler should hold up his knee so that the dog collides with it. In this way the dog learns to associate the command with a heavy impact. The association is strengthened by repetition, until finally the words alone will suffice to stop the dog in its tracks.

The same words of command and method of instruction are used to prevent a dog from jumping on to furniture. While few people will wish to entertain a muddy dog on their lounge suite it is only fair that the animal should have a comfortable basket in which to sleep. It is very useful if the dog can be taught to go to its basket on command. If the dog returns from a walk wet or muddy it can be despatched there to dry off. It can also be banished to its basket when it is making a nuisance of itself. To teach a dog this command is very easy. The handler simply places the dog in its bed at the same time repeating the word 'basket'. If the animal stays put, it is warmly praised. If it leaves its basket it is returned forcibly and the command reiterated in harsher tones. The handler should avoid the error of inconsistency. Every time the animal is allowed to disregard his command it will become less willing to respond on subsequent occasions.

Finally, it is very important, especially if one has neighbours, that a dog can be left alone without its disturbing the peace. Once again prevention is more effective than cure. A puppy whose upbringing did not involve constant attention is less likely to be a problem in this respect. Yet even a confirmed barker may be cured with a little firmness. The handler should leave the offending animal alone in its kennel (or in a spare room) for about five minutes. If the animal is quiet until he returns he should make a tremendous fuss of it. Then, next day, he should try leaving it for ten minutes. If, however, the dog starts barking before his return he should quietly creep up behind its kennel. When the dog is in full cry he should throw open the kennel door and give the animal a firm shaking (or a beating with a rolled-up newspaper). As he opens the kennel door he should shout 'be quiet' as loudly and fiercely as possible — the whole intention being to give the dog the shock of its life. After a little practice the dog will associate barking with a very nasty experience. At this stage the handler may find himself able to leave the animal for a peaceful five minutes and return to lavish praise upon it. Now he should progressively increase the length of the dog's enforced isolation (returning to silence it whenever necessary) until at last the animal is cured of its anti-social habit.

At an early age a puppy should be introduced to its collar and lead. Its first experience of lead work should be brief and happy. The dog should be taken for a five minute walk, through quiet roads to the local park. On arrival it should be allowed to run free to its heart's content. In this way the dog will come to associate lead work with a pleasant experience. Eventually the mere sight of its lead will cause the animal to bound with delight. Once the dog is accustomed to walking on a collar and lead it should be taught to do so without pulling. The lead of a well trained dog should hang slackly between the animal and its handler, neither of whom experiences the slightest discomfort. When the dog will lead gently along quiet roads it should be taught to behave in the same way on crowded pavements of busy streets. Correct leading is an essential preliminary to the exercise 'walking to heel', discussed in the following chapter.

A dog will only be dissuaded from tightening its lead if the action can be shown to have unpleasant consequences. Whenever the dog pulls, its handler should respond by jerking roughly on the lead. This jerk should be of sufficient force to cause the animal a certain amount of discomfort. A conventional collar will be quite adequate for the training of a small, placid dog. But rather more drastic measures are necessary to cause any inconvenience to a larger, more boisterous animal. Here a slip collar, often misleadingly termed a choke chain, proves invaluable. Despite the rather unfortunate nomenclature a slip collar will not choke a dog, nor harm the animal in any way unless incorrectly put on. A dog, remember, is extremely well protected and highly insensitive in the region of its throat. The sole function of this device is to constrict the neck of a violently pulling dog. The animal can terminate its discomfort whenever it wishes: by ceasing to tug! Immediately the dog stops pulling a correctly applied slip collar will automatically loosen. There are, however, two different ways in which a slip collar may be worn. Correctly fitted it slackens instantaneously. Incorrectly fitted it does not. It is vital, therefore, that when a dog owner first purchases a slip collar he should ask the retailer to demonstrate its application.

A dog should always be kept on a slack lead. It was emphasised in Chapter 3 that the handler should resist the temptation to draw his pet towards him when in the presence of strange dogs since tightening the lead only serves to inform the dog of its handler's nervousness. It is hardly surprising that the dog becomes somewhat apprehensive, too; quite probably it will endeavour to conceal its nervousness by indulging in a display of aggression. Not unnaturally any strange dog (that previously may have been quietly minding its own business) will feel itself obliged to return the challenge. Before long the handler may have a fight on his hands — the very thing he was hoping to avoid!

Use should be made of a collar and lead when teaching the dog to sit. The dog should be made to walk on a slack lead, at the handler's left side. The handler should pass the lead across the front of his body and hold the end in his right hand. When he gives the command 'sit' he should press the dog's haunches firmly to the ground using his left hand. Simultaneously he should tighten the lead with his right hand and gently pull the dog's head upwards. In addition to stopping the dog from moving away this action prevents it from folding its front legs and lying down. When the dog is in the sitting position the handler should loosen the lead and remove his left hand from the animal's rump. At this juncture he should praise the dog gently (if his praise were too lavish the animal would become excited and abandon the sitting position). If the dog shows any inclination to relinquish the sitting position the handler should push his rump down, pull its head up, and repeat the command in firm tones. When the training session is over the dog should be praised warmly and perhaps given a biscuit or two. Once the handler is sure that the dog understands what is required of it the animal should be treated to a little more discipline. Bad habits should not be allowed to develop. If the animal shows any reluctance to obey the command it should be given a sharp smack on the rump. If the dog insists on leaning lazily against the handler's legs he should knock it away with his knee. And if the dog is a tired creature that continually drops into the lying position the handler may remedy this by treading, lightly of course, upon the animal's toes. The dog will withdraw them by straightening its legs, and in so doing it automatically reassumes the sitting position.

7
FURTHER TRAINING

If it is intended to teach a dog both to sit and to lie down the commands are best taught in the order stated. If the dog first learns to lie down difficulties arise when teaching it to sit. Most dogs, being sensible creatures, are much more comfortable lying down than they are sitting — and a very convincing job they make of confusing the two instructions! A dog should be made to lie down instantly it is told to do so. The command can then be used, for example, to stop a dog from running into the road, to prevent it from chasing livestock, or to rescue any tradesman who incurs the animal's wrath.

A collar and lead are used to teach a dog to lie down. As the command is given the dog's neck is pulled downwards with the lead. With its neck in this position there is only one way that the animal can be comfortable. The dog lies down. An alternative method, useful with a powerful or stubborn dog, is for the handler to pass the lead under the instep of his shoe. Then, as he utters the command, he pulls sharply upwards on the handle of the lead. The dog's neck is pulled firmly to the ground. After a little practice the dog will associate the command 'lie down' with a rather unpleasant downward jerk. It will hurriedly adopt the recumbent position in an effort to anticipate the tug on the lead. With regular practice the dog will obey the command as a conditioned reflex. The dog's compliance should be rewarded with gentle praise: if the handler praises it too lavishly the animal will leap excitedly to its feet. At this stage the collar and lead may be dispensed with. It now remains to teach the dog to accept the command even when it is at a distance from its handler. Some dogs have no difficulty grasping this point, others insist on rejoining their handler before doing his bidding. Kim fell into the latter category. I cured her of this fault by practising the exercise whilst separated from her by a tall wire fence. First I stood close beside her and made her obey the command. Then I backed away from the fence and repeated the exercise at progressively greater ranges. In this way she grew accustomed to obeying the command at a distance; eventually she would do so without the restraining influence of the fence.

The command 'stay' is very useful. A dog that understands this instruction can be made to stop in its basket, to remain in the back of a car, or to await its handler while he visits a place where dogs are unwelcome. The exercise is best taught with the dog on a collar and lead. The dog is made to sit or lie down and the handler stands facing it holding the end of the lead. He then repeats the command 'stay' at the same time backing two or three feet away from the dog to the lead's length. If the dog moves to follow him the handler returns it, quite roughly, to its original position. At the same time he tells it to 'stay' in a firm voice. Initially this exercise is best practised indoors where there are fewer distractions to upset the dog's concentration. Up till now a collar and lead have been employed to ensure that the dog is under complete control. The next step is quietly to put the lead down beside the dog and repeat the exercise. Ultimately the dog must be taught to stay without the psychological deterrent of wearing a collar and lead. In the early stages the handler should always terminate this exercise by returning to his dog. If he finishes by calling the dog to rejoin him the animal will be constantly seeking an excuse to anticipate the recall. It is a good plan always to end with the phrase 'that'll do': until the dog hears these words it can have no possible excuse for relinquishing its vigil. The 'stay' is an exercise that readily lends itself to practice around the house. The dog can be made to stay at the far end of the kitchen while the handler washes up or, better still, in a corner of the

FURTHER TRAINING

lounge while its master sips a postprandial drink. If the animal loses its concentration it should be addressed with sharp words and hustled roughly back into its original position. By now the dog should accept the command outdoors as well as in the house. It should be sufficiently well drilled to ignore any distracting sights and smells that the outside world has to offer. Finally the dog should be taught to stay when its handler is out of its sight. This is best practised by the handler hiding himself behind a bush or tree and observing the dog's reactions whilst unseen by the animal. Any lapse by the dog should receive immediate, rigorous correction. The exercise should be practised until the dog will stay, out of sight of its master, for several minutes at a time.

The previous chapter outlined the method by which a dog may be taught to walk correctly on a collar and lead. The logical progression is to teach the dog to walk to heel, both on and off the lead. Military and police dog handlers always walk their dogs to heel on their left hand side. This leaves the right hand (weapon hand) unencumbered. It is also customary to walk the dog on the handler's left in obedience competitions. So unless the handler has any compelling reason for doing otherwise he might just as well train the dog to walk to heel on his left. The exercise is commenced with the dog, wearing a slip collar and lead, sitting with its head alongside the handler's left leg. (Whenever the handler comes to a halt he orders the dog into the sitting position). The handler holds the end of the lead in his right hand and the slack of the lead, which passes loosely across the front of his body, in his left. He gives the command 'heel' and walks forward. The dog should follow the handler maintaining its station with its head beside his left leg. If the dog moves away from the handler he should use correction or encouragement—depending upon whether the dog is being wilfully disobedient or is simply ignorant of what is required of it—to return the animal to his side. Both are dispensed with the left hand. To correct the dog the handler gives a very sharp pull on that part of the lead that

FURTHER TRAINING

stretches across in front of his body. To encourage the animal he snaps his fingers and fondles its head and muzzle. When the dog is familiar with the command and can be relied upon to maintain a slack lead it is ready to learn to walk to heel without a collar and lead. The first step is to leave the animal's collar intact but to substitute a piece of light string for its lead. By this means the dog feels quite unrestricted, but if it strays from the handler's side it can be pulled back with the string. Next the animal should be made to walk to heel wearing its collar only, without a lead of any sort. To the dog this feels exactly the same as wearing its collar with a piece of light string attached. With any luck it will walk obediently at the handler's left side. If the dog should decide to bolt the handler may, if he is sufficiently alert, snatch hold of its collar and drag it roughly back to his side. Eventually the dog should be taught to walk to heel without either a collar or a lead. At first the exercise should be practised in quiet surroundings with few distractions, but finally complete obedience should be insisted upon among crowds of people and in the vicinity of other dogs. If the dog shows any tendency to edge ahead of the handler's left calf the habit may be cured by tapping the animal lightly on its nose with a rolled-up newspaper.

Learning to work to a whistle is an essential part of the training of gun-dogs, sheepdogs, and certain military dogs. It is also very useful if a pet dog will respond to a whistle—particularly if the animal is in the habit of wandering far afield—since the whistle has a far greater range than the human voice. Training is very simple. For example the handler may wish his dog to return to him on receipt of a certain whistle note. An essential prerequisite is to train the dog to come in response to the vocal command 'come here' (see previous chapter). When the vocal command has been completely mastered the whistle should be introduced. Whenever the handler desires his dog's return he should precede the phrase 'come here' with the chosen whistle. Eventually, after continual and regular practice, the dog will associate the whistle with the command 'come here', and will return as soon as it hears the whistle without waiting for the verbal instruction. A stubborn dog may sometimes ignore the whistle. If the handler feels sure that the animal knows what is required of it the whistle should be followed by the verbal command — shouted loudly and harshly.

The same principle is used to teach a dog to work to hand signals. Hand signals, frequently employed by handlers of police and military dogs, enable dog and handler to work together in complete silence. Their obvious disadvantage is that they are valueless at night and whenever the dog is out of sight of its handler. The handler may require his dog to lie down when he holds his hand above his head. First of all he must teach the animal to obey the verbal command 'lie down'. This done he should give the verbal instruction and simultaneously raise his hand. After sufficient practice the dog will come to associate the hand signal with the words 'lie down'. When it sees the raised hand it will straight away drop to the ground anticipating the verbal command.

Occasionally a handler may have reason to teach his dog to stand. The stand is an essential part of certain obedience competitions and is a useful skill for a sheepdog to have at its disposal (see following chapter). To teach the exercise the handler employs the method described in chapter 4. Taking the scruff of the animal's neck in one hand, placing the other under its belly, he lifts his dog firmly into an upright posture; simultaneously voicing the command 'stand up', and on receipt of the command adopts the standing position.

The urge to retrieve is to a certain extent a natural canine instinct. After making a kill a wild dog often carries its victim back to its den. It does so for one of two reasons. It may prefer to eat in the security of its den, or the food may be intended for its mate who remains at home nursing a young family. Every domestic dog shows some vestige of the retrieving instinct. Hence the first step in training a dog to retrieve is simply to encourage the development of its natural desire.

Plate 16 Teaching Debbie, the Dobermann to sit

Plate 17 Debbie sitting neatly at heel

Plate 18 Heel, wearing slip collar and lead

FURTHER TRAINING

This may be achieved by playing ball with the animal, by throwing sticks for it, or by allowing it to run around carrying an old glove or slipper. At this stage retrieving should be a game—too much discipline may stifle the animal's natural instinct. A word of caution, though. The dog should be allowed to carry balls, sticks, slippers, gloves, toys and so on to its heart's content. The handler should, however, do his utmost to prevent the animal from chewing its playthings. A dog should not chew the articles it retrieves; bad habits must not be allowed to develop. When the dog will play happily with its ball and toys a proper retrieve may be attempted. To practice this exercise the handler should make or purchase a wooden dumb-bell. A correctly executed retrieve proceeds as follows. The dog sits at its handler's left side while he throws the dumb-bell. It does not immediately pursue the dumb-bell but awaits the command 'fetch it', or, 'hold it'. On receipt of the command the animal goes straight after the dumb-bell, picks it up, and returns directly to the handler. The handler makes the dog sit facing him, then gives the command 'leave' and removes the dumb-bell from the animal's mouth. Finally he gives the command 'heel'. The dog moves forward past his right leg, goes round behind him, and finally arrives alongside his left leg where it adopts the sitting position.

It would be miraculous if the dog were to perform a retrieve like this at its first attempt as there are so many mistakes that it can make. Firstly, the handler will probably find that the dog will not stay at his side when he throws the dumb-bell, but sets off after it before the command 'fetch it' is given. To prevent this the handler should tell the dog to stay, in the firmest possible voice, just before he throws the dumb-bell. If the dog is persistently disobedient the handler should put it on a collar and lead. When it rushes after the dumb-bell it should be jerked roughly back and made to await the command 'fetch it'. Another common fault is for the dog to chase the dumb-bell, to 'worry' it, but to refuse actually to pick it up One way of alleviating this problem is regularly to throw

FURTHER TRAINING

sticks, balls and so on for the dog to chase; to continually encourage the development of the animal's retrieving instinct. If the dog still refuses to take the dumb-bell in its mouth it should be taught the command 'hold it'. The handler carefully levers open the dog's mouth with his fingers and inserts the dumb-bell. He then rubs the animal's chin to prevents its jaw from falling open. As he does so he repeats the command 'hold it'. Simultaneously he encourages the dog by scratching its chest with his free hand. The next step is for the handler to hold the dumb-bell a couple of inches away from the dog's mouth and give the command. When the animal reaches out and takes the dumb-bell it is praised enthusiastically. Next the dumb-bell is held six inches from the dog's mouth, then twelve inches, then eighteen, and finally it is placed on the ground. If the dog refuses to take hold of the dumb-bell a mild form of compulsion can be employed whereby the animal's head is pushed gently down towards the dumb-bell.

A third common fault is for the dog to pursue the dumb-bell when instructed, to take hold of it, but to refuse to return with it to the handler. One way of preventing this fault is to teach the exercise indoors. In the house the dog's attention is less likely to be distracted and there is a greater chance of the animal returning when its handler calls. Another remedy is for the handler to wait until the dog has grasped the dumb-bell and then to move away from it, into another room perhaps. Usually the dog will chase after the handler bringing the dumb-bell with it. If all else fails the exercise should be practised with the dog on a collar and a long lead. If the dog will not return of its own volition the handler can compel it to do so by hauling on the lead.

Yet another fault is for the dog to fetch the dumb-bell to its handler and then to refuse to release it. The dog must be taught the command 'leave'. One way to teach this command is to force open the dog's jaws with the fingers of one hand and to extract the dumb-bell with the other. At the same time the word 'leave' is repeated. If the handler feels sure that the dog

FURTHER TRAINING

understands what is required he should try tapping it lightly on the nose as he gives the command. Very often the surprise of the blow will cause the dog to open its mouth.

The obedience exercise termed 'scent identification' is based on the retrieve. Several articles identical in appearance, handkerchiefs perhaps, are placed on the ground. Another identical article is first handled by the competition's judge and then positioned amongst them. At this juncture the dog is brought onto the scene. The judge holds out his hand for the dog to sniff and the animal is then instructed to retrieve. The dog should sniff all the articles until it detects the judge's body scent: it should return with the article that the judge handled and no other. I started to teach Kim this exercise using ten little wooden discs. One of these discs, which I could identify by a small spot of ink, I handled regularly. The other nine I avoided touching (my wife would position them for me). The discs were placed in a line with mine amongst them. I let Kim sniff my hands then walked her up to the discs on a collar and lead. At this point I gave the command 'fetch it'. I allowed her to sniff all the discs but if she picked up one of the wrong ones I would say 'no' and jerk lightly on the lead to make her drop it. When she sniffed at the disc I had handled I would say 'good girl' very enthusiastically. If she picked it up I praised her warmly. Kim quickly learned to identify my body scent, and was soon retrieving the required disc without the assistance of a collar and lead. The next step would have been to teach Kim to identify and retrieve articles handled by other people — a task I am sure she would have swiftly mastered. Yet as I am training Kim for sheepdog trials, not obedience competitions, I never troubled to progress to this stage. Debbie one day perhaps?

8
THE SHEEPDOG

A book on dog training would be incomplete without reference to one of the specialised branches of the subject. Possible topics include police dogs, military dogs, gun dogs, obedience training, tracker dogs, guide dogs for the blind and even circus dogs. I intend, however, to devote my last chapter to the sphere of dog training that I, personally, find the most fascinating — the training of working sheepdogs. An experienced trainer of gun, obedience and delinquent dogs once remarked to me that the rapport between a shepherd and his dog was absolute 'magic'. He subsequently confessed that he knew nothing at all about the training of sheepdogs. Indeed the relationship between a trained sheepdog and an experienced handler does appear somewhat mystical. In actual fact the training of these dogs is surprisingly straightforward — the basic principles have already been considered in some detail earlier in this book. Anyone with a reasonable amount of dog sense, and a couple of hundred spare hours, is perfectly capable of training a sheepdog to trial standards. (The reason this hobby is not more widespread is that few people are fortunate enough to have available the sheep with which to train a dog and the space in which to do so.)

Much, of course, depends on the dog. However excellent and industrious the handler he will enjoy little success if his dog does not possess a measure of natural ability. Border collies are used for working sheep since dogs of this strain have the two invaluable qualities of intelligence and a highly developed herding instinct. So strong is this instinct that it frequently manifests itself in a dog that has received no training whatsoever, a dog that has never encountered a sheep in its life. Quite often a pet collie will round up a flock of chickens, ducks or geese and herd them unerringly towards its astonished owner. Unfortunately the inheritance of this instinct is somewhat unpredictable. Of a litter of six from well bred working parents it is not uncommon for two of the puppies to show no interest at all in sheep. The instinct remains dormant.

Herding is a sublimation of the hunting instinct, as explained in Chapter 2, and a sheepdog's style of working is direct evidence of the close relationship between the two instincts. A sheepdog's 'eye' and gait are strikingly similar to the bearing of a cat stalking a bird, or a fox stealing up on a rabbit. The dog will fix the sheep with a steady gaze, and move slowly and purposefully towards them. Sheep, like all herbivorous animals, have an instinctive dread of carnivores and will inevitably move away at the dog's approach. A sheepdog loves to work because, in so doing, it is fulfilling an innate urge — the hunting instinct. It only takes a whisper to encourage a collie to work, though considerable firmness may be required to recall the animal when its task is completed.

A sheepdog's mode of working stems from the animal's hunting instinct. For this reason a young untrained Border collie is not above biting or harassing a sheep which is, of course, most undesirable. To have his dog under complete control the handler must first of all train the animal to lie down instantly it receives his command: no matter where it is, no matter what it is doing. The dog should be taught to lie down before it ever sets eye on a sheep (see previous chapter). When the young dog is one hundred per cent obedient, and only then, it is ready for its first introduction to sheep. It should be taken into a field containing a few docile ewes and its reactions observed. If it shows no interest training can proceed no further; the handler must wait a few weeks and then repeat the experiment. If, however, the young animal shows some 'eye' it should be encouraged enthusiastically. As the dog instinctively stalks the sheep the handler should repeat the words 'walk on'. Occasionally he should give the command 'lie down'. Very likely the command will be ignored; the dog is concentrating so hard on the sheep that the words do not even register on its brain. In this case the command should be repeated in a louder, harsher voice. If, after several repetitions, the dog still refuses to accept the command it should be put on a collar and lead. The handler should keep the lead very slack as the dog advances on the sheep. Periodically he should give the command 'lie down'; if the dog refuses to obey he should jerk it to the ground with the lead. By this means the dog will quickly learn to accept the command as readily as it did in its preliminary training. With sufficient practice the dog will come to associate the words 'walk on' with its instinctive stalking of the sheep. If ever it chooses to disregard them it may be directed towards the sheep with a tug on the lead. Eventually the dog should be able to advance on a flock of sheep, off the lead, alternately accepting the commands 'lie down' and 'walk on'. Once the animal is word perfect its training may proceed a step further.

Two words of caution: firstly the handler should avoid putting his dog into a situation where a sheep might turn on it. The young animal should be trained on sheep that have been well 'dogged' and should never be used to force stubborn sheep into a tight corner. A young sheepdog is very impressionable. If during its puppyhood it is exposed to the attacks of an angry ewe it will lose its self-confidence. This will have an adverse effect on the dog's entire working career. Secondly the handler should never allow his dog to bite a sheep. Fortunately it is easy to anticipate when a dog is about to grip because it rushes in with tail held high; as soon as the handler sees this he should shout 'lie down' in the severest tones. If the dog does not respond it should be given further practice on a collar and lead. The handler should persist until the dog accepts the command as a conditioned reflex; until it automatically obeys irrespective of its state of mind. Even a moderately experienced dog will sometimes bite a sheep. Such behaviour should not pass unremarked and the handler must dispense an immediate verbal lashing, though physical punishment is not to be recommended except with a confirmed biter. Rough treatment may cause a young dog with a poorly developed working instinct to lose all interest in sheep.

When the sheep first come into view at the start of a training session the handler should tell his dog to 'see'. After a little practice the word will cause the dog to come alert and scan the locality for sheep. At the end of a session the handler should call his dog and as it rather reluctantly takes leave of the sheep he should repeat the phrase 'that'll do'. These two commands, 'see' and 'that'll do', are used by handlers at sheepdog trials at the commencement and conclusion of their runs.

The next step is to teach the two commands that direct the dog to its right and its left respectively. The distinction between right and left is quite an advanced concept for the canine intellect and the teaching of this exercise will require several months of regular, patient practice. Different handlers use different words to direct their dogs right and left. The commands themselves are immaterial provided that they are brief, clear and individually distinct. I use the word 'away' to direct Kim to her right and 'bye' to direct her to her left. There are several ways of teaching these commands: all make use of the dog's instinct to herd the sheep to its handler. One method is for the handler to position himself and his dog so that they are facing one another from opposite sides of a flock of about half a dozen sheep. The handler now walks backwards, in a straight line, at the same time instructing his dog to 'walk on'. The dog's advance compels the sheep to follow the handler — thus dog, sheep and handler maintain their relative positions. So far all is quite straightforward; the dog has only to advance in a straight line to hold the sheep to its handler. But what if the handler were to describe a curved path? Imagine the handler bearing to his left as he walks backwards. If the dog were to continue walking in a straight line it would no longer be directing the sheep towards its handler (they would, in fact, be straying off to the handler's right). This, of course, conflicts with the dog's herding instinct and it will automatically move to its left so that it is again holding the sheep to its handler. As the dog moves left the handler should repeat the command 'bye'. When dog and sheep have regained their former positions relative to the handler he should continue to walk backwards in a straight line. Next he should bear to his right as he walks backwards so that the dog is required to move to its right to herd the sheep to him. As it does so he should repeat the command 'away'. After weeks of regular practice the dog will come to associate the command 'bye' with moving to its left and 'away' with moving to its right. Now the handler should try standing well back from the flock and directing the dog right and left without giving it the benefit of any instinctive clues. If the dog obeys a command it should be praised warmly. If it mistakes its right and its left the handler should make it aware of its error by shouting 'no' in a fierce voice.

Once a young collie has learned to accept the commands 'left', 'right', 'lie down' and 'walk on' it has some sort of claim to being a sheepdog.

To move sheep with a dog the shepherd must position the animal on the opposite side of the flock to that in which he wishes it to move. Then, as the dog advances, the sheep are forced in the required direction.

Using these four commands the handler can position his dog anywhere round the circumference of a flock then call it forward. But before a dog realises its full potential as a farm worker, and before it is ready to enter even a novice sheepdog trial, it must be taught to gather—to collect a flock of sheep from several hundred yards away and fetch them to its handler. This exercise is taught in a series of easy steps. At first the handler stands close to the flock and directs his dog either right or left until it is diametrically opposite him on the far side of the flock. He stops the dog at this point and then instructs him to walk forward. Now the handler repeats the exercise standing ten yards from the flock. He sends his dog, stops it at the 'twelve o'clock' position, then calls it forward. The dog fetches the sheep to its handler. When the dog is competent over ten yards the range is increased to twenty yards, to fifty yards and so on, until finally the dog is gathering from distances of a quarter of a mile or more. Between leaving the handler and arriving at the rear of the sheep the dog passes one of the flanks of the flock. It is important that when it does so, it skirts the sheep as widely as possible; if it makes the mistake of running too close to the flock the sheep may bolt in a sideways direction (away from the dog.) In a correct gather the sheep remain undisturbed and stationary until the dog is at the 'twelve o'clock' position. Then the dog advances fetching the sheep to the handler in as straight a line as possible. In training of this sort regularity is paramount; five or ten minutes *every* day should be the target. Exceed this figure and there is a danger of the dog's becoming 'stale' and losing all interest in sheep.

A sheepdog may be trained for either or both of two reasons: to compete in sheepdog trials or to facilitate the handling of livestock on the farm. Some dogs excel in both spheres. Often, though, a trial dog is not at its best on the farm, and a farm dog is somewhat out of its depth at a sheepdog trial, since the everyday routine of a farm dog is not at all comparable to the very specialised requirements of a sheepdog trial course.

From the reader's point of view, it is easier to appreciate the training routine for a sheepdog trial. The activities of a farm dog vary greatly from farm to farm, and from handler to handler, besides which few people have the opportunity to observe a farm dog in action. The routine for trials, however, is the same everywhere and anyone can attend one. Furthermore, it is a simple matter to describe the standardised layout of a trial course and the very precise rules for its negotiation.

THE SHEEPDOG

Look at the diagram of the National course as defined by the International Sheepdog Society (opposite). The majority of local societies run their trials over this course — sometimes a rather shorter version due to lack of available space. Many societies additionally provide a small, simplified course for the benefit of novice dogs and handlers. The National course, which is scored out of one hundred points, is commenced at post 1. Dog and handler wait here while five sheep are positioned alongside post 2. The two posts are four hundred yards apart. The handler sends his dog either right or left to gather the sheep. The outrun, or cast, is marked out of twenty points. It should be pear-shaped and the dog should not stop until it is exactly behind the sheep. After sending his dog the handler is not permitted to leave post 1, and points are deducted if he has reason to redirect the dog before it reaches the 'twelve o'clock' position.

The next operation is known as the lift. In a correct lift the dog halts or slows down exactly behind the sheep and then advances smoothly and cautiously. It does not rush in at the sheep, neither does it hang back requiring numerous commands. The sheep remain stationary and undisturbed until the dog's advance eases them gently towards the handler. Ten marks are awarded for a perfect lift. From this point onwards the continuous line on the diagram depicts the path of the sheep as guided by the dog. The path of the dog itself is unimportant provided the sheep follow the correct line. In actual fact the dog will normally be positioned about five or ten yards behind the sheep. The dog's guiding of the sheep from post 2 to the handler at post 1 is termed the fetch. The fetch should be in as straight a line as possible and should pass between a pair of hurdles (marked A in diagram) seven yards apart and one hundred and fifty yards from the handler. The fetch is marked out of twenty points, and for each sheep that fails to pass through the fetch gates a minimum of half a point will be deducted. The dog that uses its initiative and requires the fewest commands will be preferred.

THE SHEEPDOG

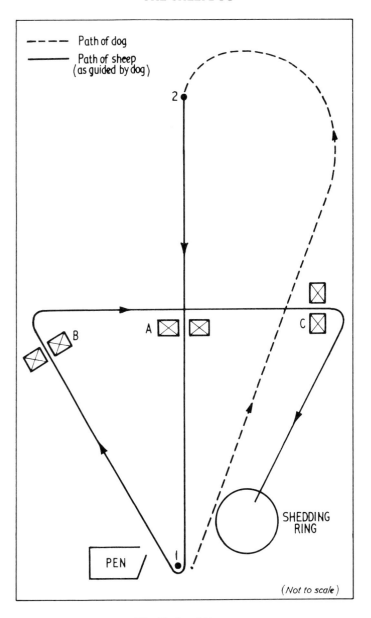

The National Course

THE SHEEPDOG

On completion of the fetch the sheep should pass round behind the handler, as close to him as possible, and straight into the drive. The drive takes the form of a triangle with post 1, and hurdles B and C at its corners. Each side of the triangle measures 150yd making a tótal drive of four hundred and fifty yards. The sides of the triangle should be kept as straight as possible and the dog should steadily follow the sheep keeping them moving gently the whole time. The drive is marked out of twenty points and points will be deducted for a dog that continually stops or that moves the sheep at an excessive speed. In addition, for each sheep that misses either of the pairs of drive gates a minimum of half a point will be deducted. The handler who gives the fewest, quietest commands will be awarded the highest score. This last rule applies to all aspects of sheepdog trialing.

The completion of the drive should put the sheep into the shedding ring — a circle twenty-five yards in diameter marked on the ground. Only when the sheep are all inside the shedding ring may the handler leave post 1. Of the five sheep three are unmarked and two are marked, the latter having coloured string round their necks or indelible pencil on the back of their heads. The dog must separate two of the unmarked sheep and drive them away under complete control; for so doing it is awarded ten points. Keeping the sheep inside the shedding ring, handler and dog manoeuvre themselves on opposite sides of the flock, waiting until the slightest gap appears between two of the required sheep and the other three. When such a gap does appear the handler calls his dog into it and the sheep split. The handler then directs his dog to drive off the two unmarked sheep. During this operation the handler is not permitted to touch the sheep neither is he permitted to split the sheep himself (by leaping into the gap). The shed must be performed by the dog and the dog alone.

Following successful completion of the shed the dog allows the sheep to reunite. Meanwhile the handler walks to the pen which is constructed of hurdles and measures six feet by nine feet. At one end is a six foot gate with six feet of rope attached to it. The handler opens the gate, takes hold of the end of the rope, and directs the dog to bring the sheep up to him. The dog now works the sheep into the pen whilst the handler, with rope in one hand and crook in the other, essays to prevent them from bolting. Ten points are awarded for penning. Points are deducted for every failure to pen—that is, every time the sheep bolt. Points are also lost if the handler touches a sheep with the gate while closing it. After penning the handler releases the sheep and resecures the pen gate (failure to do so results in the deduction of points). Then dog, sheep and handler proceed once again to the shedding ring for an exercise termed the single. The dog has to shed a single marked sheep from the other four and prevent it from rejoining them; successfully accomplished it is awarded ten points. As in shedding it is most important that the dog, and not the handler, splits the sheep and drives the single away. Once the single is accomplished the course is completed. The maximum possible score is one hundred points and the time limit for the entire operation is fifteen minutes.

When training a dog to negotiate the course it is preferable if the dog works to a whistle as well as to vocal commands (see previous chapter), mainly because the course is so long. A proper shepherd's whistle fits right inside the mouth and can emit varying notes as well as a straight blast. It is common to use four different codes for 'lie down', 'walk on', 'right' and 'left'; many handlers give one blast for 'lie down', two blasts for 'walk on', and employ two different distinct notes to direct their dogs left and right.

The importance of starting with short casts and progressively increasing their length can never be over-emphasised. Many dogs lose points because their casts are too shallow. Instead of running out wide and leaving the sheep undisturbed until reaching the 'twelve o'clock' position, they displace the sheep laterally before ever reaching their rear. A cast of this sort invariably results in a ragged start to the fetch. The help of an assistant is very useful to cure this fault. He (or she) should stand in the bulge of the pear (see p. 99) and ensure that the dog passes outside him on its outrun. Another common fault is for a dog to stop short (before 'twelve o'clock', that is) on its cast. Whenever it stops short in training the handler should shout the initial command, 'bye' or 'away', in an angry voice. As the dog responds by continuing to move left or right it should be praised. When the dog reaches the 'twelve o'clock' position, or slightly beyond, it is stopped with the 'lie down' whistle. Short casts should be practised at first so that the dog is under strict control; when the bad habit is cured the length of cast may be progressively increased.

There are only two mistakes that a dog can make on its lift; to approach the sheep too fast, or to approach them too slowly. The former error is by far the more common. Again the remedy is to practise short casting, where rigorous discipline can be applied, and to insist that the dog lies down and stays down when the stop whistle is given. When the dog is completely reliable on a short cast the length of cast may be gradually increased.

In the fetch a dog is fulfilling its herding instinct and naturally endeavours to bring the sheep to its handler in as straight a line as possible. Thus it is important not to overcommand a dog when practising fetching because in this case it will never learn to use its own initiative. A dog that advances steadily on its fetch, remaining on its feet the whole time, is preferable to one that alternately rushes forward and then lies down. In the former case the sheep move smoothly, in the latter case they progress in a series of bursts and halts. It is a considerable advantage in this respect if the dog can be taught to respond to the command 'steady'. It is also useful to teach the dog to stand up on command, as described in the previous chapter. If the dog can come to a halt while staying on its feet the sheep are less likely to stop moving than if it claps itself to the ground

THE SHEEPDOG

The best method of teaching a dog to pen is by continual practice using different sheep whenever possible. Individual sheep vary greatly in their response to the proceedings. Some bolt, some stand immobile ignoring dog and handler alike, some break away from their fellows, and some — all too few alas — just wander quietly into the pen. It is important, therefore, that the dog should accumulate experience of as many different types of sheep as possible. After a while the dog realises what is required of it and uses its own initiative to hold the sheep to the pen.

Casting, lifting, fetching and penning are logical extensions of the dog's early training. The animal is not required to grasp any new concept. Driving and shedding, however, are fundamentally different from the disciplines listed above. Both are very unnatural for a dog because both conflict with the animal's natural instincts. A dog instinctively fetches the sheep to its handler; but driving requires precisely the opposite course of action. A dog instinctively herds the sheep into a flock; yet shedding requires it to divide them into smaller units. Because of this the dog finds these two exercises the most difficult and they are not taught until the animal has a firm grasp of the rudiments of its work. For the same reason driving and shedding are not normally included in novice sheepdog trial courses.

Only when the handler is convinced that his dog has a sound knowledge of the four basic commands should he start to teach it to drive. Dog and handler stand together facing a flock of sheep. The dog is told to 'walk on' and as it advances the sheep begin to move away from the handler. At this stage the dog may be tempted to rush off and herd them back. If it does so the handler should give the command 'lie down' very emphatically. When the dog is back under control he should once again direct it to 'walk on'. The dog will follow the sheep with growing reluctance for a maximum of about ten yards. At this point it will probably come to a complete halt refusing to drive any further. In such a situation all the handler can do is to

THE SHEEPDOG

recall his dog and to try again the following day. Next day the dog will be a little more familiar with the proceedings and will drive for perhaps twelve yards. A couple of weeks of regular practice will increase the animal's range to something like twenty yards. Now the dog must be taught to move to its right and left while driving, so that it can be positioned to direct the sheep through the drive gates. Often the dog's herding instinct will cause it to edge off to one or other side in an effort to head the sheep back to its handler. If, for example, the dog moves left—to its own left, to the handler's left, and along the left flank of the flock—the handler should stop it with the command 'lie down'. He should then prevent the sheep from deviating to their right by calling the dog 'away'. If the dog accepts the command all well and good. Often, though, the dog will show signs of confusion because the command conflicts with its herding instinct. If the dog's confusion causes it to mistake the command, to move further left instead of right, the handler should shout 'no' in a loud voice. Having stopped the dog he should give the command 'come here'. The dog will move to its right to rejoin the handler. As it does so the handler should repeat the command 'away'. This will cause the animal to renew its interest in the sheep while simultaneously moving in the required direction. When the dog is behind the sheep the handler should instruct it to walk on: it will now be correctly positioned to direct the sheep through the drive gates.

To teach a dog to shed, three or four very docile sheep are needed. Nervous, excitable sheep will struggle furiously to keep themselves in a single group and holding them apart will prove too much for an inexperienced dog. Dog and handler position themselves on either side of the small flock. The handler moves forward squeezing the sheep between himself and the dog waiting for a gap to appear between, for example, two pairs of sheep. When the sheep split the handler steps smartly into the gap, at the same time giving the command 'come here'. Dog and handler meet between the sheep; the handler then directs his dog to drive away one pair of sheep. At a sheepdog trial this manoeuvre would not pass for a shed because it was the handler's advance, not the dog's, which separated the sheep. It does, however, give a young dog an idea of what shedding is all about. Once the dog knows what is required of it the handler's rôle becomes more and more passive. He stands still letting the dog work the sheep to him and awaiting the appearance of the slightest gap. When such a rift occurs his only action is to call the dog into the shed. On receipt of this single command the dog darts into the gap, splits the sheep, and then uses its own initiative to hold them apart.

In describing the practical training of a sheepdog I have here outlined the method by which I trained Kim. I do not insist that this is the best training method, neither do I maintain that it is the only one (there are as many different training techniques as there are sheepdog handlers.) My only claim is that by this process it is possible to train a sheepdog to a moderate standard of performance. If the reader cares to visit a sheepdog trial he will meet many experienced shepherds the majority of whom will be pleased to discuss their own, personal, training methods. Many of these handlers are far more experienced than I, but regrettably few of them show any inclination to go into print (and much of what they say *is* printable!). Yet if this chapter serves only to arouse the reader's interest in a truly fascinating aspect of dog training it will not have been completely wasted.

INDEX

Page numbers in italic type indicate illustrations.

Aggression, 11, 32, 35, 37-43
Alsatian, 27, 29, 68
Anthropomorphism, 53, 54, 58, 62
Anticipation; by dog, 58, 59, 82, 83, 86; by handler, 66, 67, 78
Appeasement gestures, *see* Submissive gestures
Association of ideas, 54-9, 61-71, 75, 79
Away!, 95, 96, 102

Balance of nature, 42
Barking, 17, 62, 79
Basket!, 78, 79
Be quiet!, 79
Biting (gripping), 27, 64, 66, 93-5
Biting order, 39, 45; *see also* Hierarchy
Border Collie; style of working, 28, 54, 93
Breeding, 23, 25-7, 30
Bye!, 95, 96, 102

Camouflage, 22
Cape hunting dog, 9, 10, 14, 36
Casting; by sheepdog, 64, 101-3
Cat, 14, 22, 24, 44, 45
Cave dwellers, 24
Chasing cyclists, 61
Choke chain (slip collar), 47, 65, 80, 84, *70*
Colour vision, 13
Come here!, 63, 76, 77, 85, 86
Commands, 58, 59, 95
Communication; between handler and dog, 71, 73
Consistency in training, 56, 62-4

Corgi, 28, 29
Correction of misbehaviour, 57, 60-71
Coyote, 9, 13, 36

Diet, 14-16
Dingo, 42
Discipline, 60-71
Display, *see* Gestures
Dobermann pinscher; personality of, 7, 50, 65, 68
Dog fights, 11
Dog Shows, 26
Domestication, 24, 25
Dominance, 9-11, 44-50
Dominant gestures, 11, 39, 40
Driving; by sheepdog, 103, 104
Dumb-bell, 65, 89, 90

Eating habits of wild dogs, 14-16
'Eye'; of sheepdog, 27, 58, 93, 94, *51*

Fear of dogs, 40, 41
Feeding, *see* Diet
Fetching (gathering); by sheepdog, 96-8, 102, 103
Fetch it!, 89
Fierce dogs, 40, 47
Flexibility of approach, 8, 64, 74
Flock work, 93-7
Fox, 9, 13, 14, 30, 31

Gathering (fetching); by sheepdog, 96-8, 102, 103
Genetics, 19, 20, 26, 27
Gestures, 10, 11, 18, 39, 40, 81
Get down!, 78

INDEX

Greyhound, 29
Gripping (biting), 27, 64, 66, 93-5
Guard dogs, 36, 37
Gun dogs, 30, 31

Hand signals, 86
Hearing, 13
Heel, 84, 85, *34, 87, 88*
Herding, 27, 28, 92, 93
Hierarchy, 9, 10, 39, 45, 48, 49
Hold it!, 89, 90
Hounds, 30
House training, 22, 74, 75
Howling, 17
Hunting dogs, 11-14, 25, 27-30, 93
Husky, 35

Improvisation, 7, 74
Instinct, 21, 22; burying food, 16; care of young, 17, 22; cleanliness, 22, 74; greed, 15; guarding, 36-8; herding, 27, 28, 92; hierarchical, 9, 10, 45, 48, 49; hunting 11-14, 27, 30, 61; mating, 16, 36; retrieving, 30, 65, 86; territorial, 32, 35-8
International Sheepdog Society, 29

Jackal, 9, 13, 14, 16, 17, 24, 25, 36
Jumping up, 78

Kennel Club, 29
Kennel fights, 11

Lead work, 41, 79-81, 84, 85, *87*
Learning, 53-9
Leave!, 89, 90
Licking, 18
Lie down!, 82, 83, 93, 94, 101, 103
Lifting; by sheepdog, 98, 102, 103
Lone wolf, 10
Lorenz, Konrad, 48

Marking of territory, 17, 36, 37
Marsupial wolf, 42
Mating, 16, 20, 36

Mutations, 19, 20

National Sheepdog Trial course, 98, *99*
Natural selection (survival of the fittest), 11, 19-23, 38
Night vision, 14
No!, 77, 78, 91, 96, 104
Novice sheepdog trial course, 98, 103

Obedience; classes, 72, 73; competitions, 73, 84, 91; training, 72-91
Old English sheepdog, 28, 29
Olfactory membrane, 11, 12

Pack law, 9-11, 14, 16, 20, 21, 44, 48, 49
Pavlov, Ivan, 56
Pecking order, 39, 49; *see also* Hierarchy
Pedigree breeds, 27
Penning; by sheepdog, 100, 101, 103
Practice; about the house, 74-9, 83; regularity, 57, 97
Praise, 56, 62, 71
Punishment, *see* Correction of misbehaviour
Puppy, commencement of training, 46, 74

Ratting, 30
Reasoning, 53-5
Redirected aggression, 39
Registration of Border Collie, 29
Regularity of training, 57, 97
Regurgitation, 18
Retrieving; instinct, 30, 65, 86; training, 65, 86-91, *33*

Scent; canine scenting, 11-13, 16; scent identification (obedience exercise), 91
See!, 95

INDEX

Shedding; by sheepdog, 100, 101, 103-5, *51*
Sheepdog; trials and training, 92-105
Sheep worrying, 9
Sit!, 81, *87*
Slip collar (choke chain), 47, 65, 80, 84, *70*
Smell, *see* Scent
Stand up!, 58, 86, *34*
Stay!, 83, 84; stay and recall (obedience exercise), 59, *69*
Submissive gestures, 10, 18, 40
Survival of the fittest (natural selection), 11, 19-23, 38

Terriers, 30
Territory, 17, 32, 35-8
That'll do!, 83, 95
Titbits, 63, 71, 76, 81
Tracking, 12
Trainers; professional, 72
Trials; sheepdog, 92-105
Tripe, 15

Urine; of bitch in season, 37; territory marking, 17, 36, 37

Vision, 13, 14

Walk on!, 94, 95, 101, 103
Whelping, 17
Whistle, 85, 86, 101
Wolf, 9, 14, 16, 17, 24, 25, 27, 35, 36; training of, 50, 53
Worms, 16